Pressure Canning Without the Danger

Your Comprehensive Guide to Safely Using Your Pressure Canner. With Tips, Tricks, and USDA Guidelines to Help You Use Your Pressure Canner Without Risks!

Linda C. Johnson

© Copyright 2021-All rights reserved.

The content contained within this book may not be reproduced, duplicated or transmitted without direct written permission from the author or the publisher.

Under no circumstances will any blame or legal responsibility be held against the publisher, or author, for any damages, reparation, or monetary loss due to the information contained within this book, either directly or indirectly.

Legal Notice:

This book is copyright protected. It is only for personal use. You cannot amend, distribute, sell, use, quote or paraphrase any part, or the content within this book, without the consent of the author or publisher.

Disclaimer Notice:

Please note the information contained within this document is for educational and entertainment purposes only. All effort has been executed to present accurate, up to date, reliable, complete information. No warranties of any kind are declared or implied. Readers acknowledge that the author is not engaged in the rendering of legal, financial, medical or professional advice. The content within this book has been derived from various sources. Please consult a licensed professional before attempting any techniques outlined in this book.

By reading this document, the reader agrees that under no circumstances is the author responsible for any losses, direct or indirect, that are incurred as a result of the use of the information contained within this document, including, but not limited to, errors, omissions, or inaccuracies.

Table of Contents

TABLE OF CONTENTS 4

YOUR FREE GIFTS! 1

INTRODUCTION 2

CHAPTER 1: CHOOSING YOUR PRESSURE CANNER 5
    CAN I USE A PRESSURE COOKER? 5
    CAN I USE A WATER BATH CANNER? 7
    WHICH BRAND IS BEST? 9
    DOES SIZE MATTER? 11
    OTHER CONSIDERATIONS 13

CHAPTER 2: THE PARTS OF A PRESSURE CANNER 16
    GASKET 16
    WEIGHTED GAUGE VS. DIAL GAUGE 18
    VENT PIPE 20
    OVERPRESSURE PLUG 22
    CANNING RACK 23

CHAPTER 3: PRESSURE CANNING PREPARATION 26
    CHOOSING A RECIPE 26
    PREPARING THE FOOD 28
    JAR PREPARATION 30
    FAMILIARIZE YOURSELF WITH YOUR MODEL 32
    TEST RUN 34

CHAPTER 4: HOW TO USE A PRESSURE CANNER 37
    PREPARING THE PRESSURE CANNER 37
    PRESSURIZING 39
    DEPRESSURIZING 41

Removing the Contents..43
Common Errors and How to Fix Them.....................................45

CHAPTER 5: WHAT CAN CAN AND WHAT CAN'T CAN 48

When to Use a Pressure Canner 48
Vegetable Do's and Don'ts...50
Meat Do's and Don'ts..52
Other Foods You Can Can..54
What Never to Can..55

CHAPTER 6: PRESSURE CANNING VEGETABLES...................... 58

Harvesting 58
Storing Vegetables 60
Vegetables: Raw Pack vs. Hot Pack 62
Plain Vegetables..64
Mixed Vegetables..66

CHAPTER 7: PRESSURE CANNING STOCK 68

What Is Stock?..68
The Basics of Stock Safety...70
The Benefits of Canning Stock 71
Chicken Broth vs. Beef Broth..73
Tips for Canning Broth 74

CHAPTER 8: BONUS CHAPTER - PRESSURE CANNING MEAT . 77

The Basics of Meat Safety 77
Meat: Raw Pack vs. Hot Pack 78
Meat Products 80
Poultry and Rabbit 82
Seafood..83

CHAPTER 9: CARING FOR YOUR PRESSURE CANNER 85

Basic Maintenance..85
Part Replacement 87
Cleaning 89
Caring for Utensils..91
Storing...92

CHAPTER 10: WHAT'S THE WORST THAT COULD HAPPEN?... 95
- Botulism 95
- Avoiding Contamination 97
- Understanding Food Acid Levels... 99
- Will My Pressure Canner Explode?...................................... 101
- How to Spot Danger.. 102

CONCLUSION 105

THANK YOU 108
- >> Click here to leave a review on Amazon and see my other books on Food Preservation << 108

REFERENCES 109

Your Free Gifts!

Out of all of the available literature on pressure canning safety, you chose this one. Thank you. As a way to express my gratitude, I'm offering 3 additional valuable resources for FREE to my readers.

Get instant access by going to www.customercore.eu

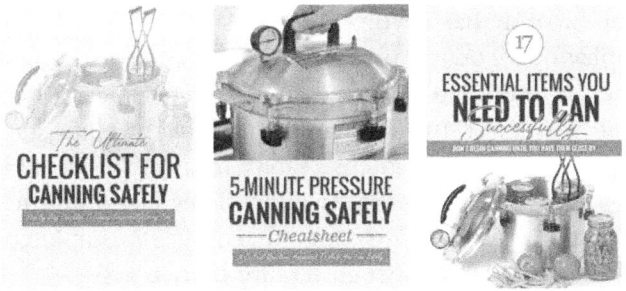

- FREE GIFT NO.1 Is My Ultimate Checklist For Canning Successfully every time.
- FREE GIFT NO.2 Is My 5-Minute Cheat Sheet To Help You Can Safely.
- FREE GIFT NO.3 Is My 17 Essential Items You Need To Can Successfully.

If you want to can safely and enjoyably, make sure to grab these 3 free resources.

Introduction

It is almost impossible to think of the pressure canner without considering its dangerous connotations. Many horror stories consisting of exploding lids and dodging boiling water have tainted the good name of the kitchen necessity. The pressure canner has been around for a long time and with that history comes the inevitable criticism. Just because your grandma's kitchen turned into an unwanted steam room doesn't mean yours will. The world has evolved and so has it's kitchen appliances. Today's pressure canners are not the faulty ones of the 1950's. Manufacturers were quick to learn that you can't make a profit if your product keeps exploding and thus intense safety measures were added to improve customer satisfaction. They just don't make them like they used to, and that is why your kitchen ceiling is safe from flying pressure canner lids.

The pressure canner, just like any other heavy equipment, should be handled with the utmost care and consideration. It is not a toaster. You can't just skim through the directions, push the on button and hope for the best. Just because this is the modern age of safety and precaution doesn't mean there haven't been any accidents. In contrast to this, it is not an impossible ten sided Rubik's cube. There is no reason to be intimidated. People have been successfully canning using a pressure canner for decades and will continue for years to come. As long as this balance of care and confidence is successfully navigated there will be no issue.

Still unsure if using a pressure canner is the right choice? Why bother canning at all when the nearest grocery store has a can of green beans for less than a dollar. There is a common misconception that simple, organic lifestyles such as canning are not as cost efficient. This misleading information stunts the growth of consumer independence from big corporations. Canning is an investment, whether it is used for business or just feeding your family. There's no doubt that pressure canners can be expensive, but so is the average monthly grocery bill. The amount of food thrown out due to spoilage is ridiculous: Hard earned money down the drain. Food prices are rising and, if the last fifty years are any indication, they are just going to get higher. Investing today saves you and your family from becoming just another victim of inflation.

Another important benefit to using a pressure canner is knowing exactly what is in your family's food. Even with F.D.A. regulations, there's no way of knowing every single ingredient that goes into the canned goods at the grocery store. With every new food related research study, it's understandable that canning would be part of a new trend. Not only are you freeing yourself from the hold that major chains have on the American family, but you are expressing the freedom of choosing what you want to eat. Whether it's no gluten, all gluten, keto friendly, paleo, or coma-inducing levels of sugar, the choice on what you eat is all yours.

Consumer liberation is an obvious choice, however, the important question still remains. Will my pressure canner explode? The answer: Probably not. That is perhaps not the most reassuring answer, but the truth is that something can go wrong: Mostly happening when we're not being safe. Even with all the technical advances in the world, the pressure canner is not foolproof. That's why this book exists, to keep the kitchen nice and tidy. Blunders will occur, but the best part about mistakes is that they never have to happen twice. Luckily, someone somewhere has already made those mistakes so now you don't have to.

This ambiguous answer might not be enough so to put it plain and simple, the pressure canner is not a dangerous appliance. A car causes far more fatalities and disasters in a year than the pressure canner could in all the time of its existence. Does that mean cars should become obsolete? Of course not. As long as everyone abides by the laws of traffic and is careful, there's no reason to fear vehicles of any kind. It's when people don't that crashes happen. The pressure canner is just as safe as you make it, and by choosing to read this book you've already proven that you're smart and capable enough to be perfectly safe.

Chapter 1:

Choosing Your Pressure Canner

Can I Use a Pressure Cooker?

No. Well, maybe. If you're making a delicious beef stew, then by all means use a pressure cooker. However, if you plan on canning that beef stew, then a pressure canner is required. Despite their similar names the two appliances are not interchangeable. Canning food is not as easy as placing it in jars and heating it up. There are many safety procedures put in place to make sure the food is safely edible. If these aren't followed, it runs the risk of dangerous toxins contaminating the canned food that can lead to serious illness and possibly death.

The confusion between these two appliances is understandable: Besides their names, pressure cookers and pressure canners have similar processes as well. Pressure being the key word. Both are sealed pots that build up pressure through the use of steam. In addition, the two contraptions have a kindred history. Cookers have the same unfortunate reputation as canners, stemming from past unsafe manufacturing errors. It was through the technology of pressure cooking, that the canning community discovered this new and safe way to can low acid foods. The canner is a modified version of the cooker, and it's main purpose is preservation rather than immediate consumption.

The other difference between the pressure canner and the pressure cookers is the size. Most pressure cookers, like the instapot, are smaller and only hold about four or less quarts. Pressure canners are larger, and are capable of canning seven quart jars or even up to 24 half pint jars at a time. This size difference completely changes the heat up and cool down process and because of this, canning in a pressure cooker can lead to an under processed result. Even the largest pressure cookers aren't capable of recreating the environment that is needed to stop contamination.

Since pressure cookers are not manufactured with the purpose of canning, they are missing integral parts to the process. Many cookers will not have gauges that measure the pressure inside the pot. Without this feature there is no way to know if the food is safe to consume. Even in the rare case that a pressure cooker does have a gauge, they are not always very reliable because the process of pressure cooking isn't as exact as pressure canning is. It is very important to know just exactly how much pressure is being put on the jars and their contents when canning.

Manufacturers may claim that their pressure cooker is safe for canning, but it's important to research further into this claim and make sure the cooker is USDA approved for pressure canning. If the cooker is smaller than 16 quarts then there is no safe way to convert canning recommendations. Even with a large enough cooker that has an adjustable gauge, most USDA approved recipes are going to call for a pressure canner to avoid any possible mistakes. Ultimately it's the customer's decision, but considering the possible deadly repercussions, I cannot recommend using a pressure cooker as a pressure canner.

Can I Use a Water Bath Canner?

No. Well maybe. A water bath canner is a perfectly valid way to can food products, unlike the pressure cooker which can be dangerous. Water bath canning is not the same thing as pressure canning, however. There are two common methods to canning due to the fact that different foods require different circumstances to be safely preserved. Pressure canning utilizes steam to create high levels of heated pressure that sterilizes the jars. Water bath canners can not reach the same temperatures and are only used for products that don't need high heat to be processed.

Unlike the pressure canner, a special water bath canner is not actually required for water bath canning. All that is needed is a large pot, a lid and a rack to hold the jars at the bottom. However, there are pots that are manufactured specifically for water bath canning. Pressure canners only use about 1-3 inches of water compared to the water bath method where the jars are completely immersed in the boiling water. Because of this, preserves in water bath canners can only reach the temperature of the water. It is during the cool down time that jars become sealed and the food within them becomes safely preserved. The time in which this takes place is usually specified in the recipe.

Knowing what type of food requires a water bath versus what type requires a pressure canner is very important. A water bath canner only reaches temperatures of 212 degrees Fahrenheit, whereas a pressure canner can heat to 240 degrees Fahrenheit. This can be the difference between enjoying delicious preserved food or suffering through food poisoning. Water bath canning is only really used for fruits, fruit products like pie filling or chutney, vinegar, and condiments. Pressure canning is for vegetables, certain kinds of meats, and broth. When following a canning recipe, make sure to double check what canning method is required.

So what is the difference between these two groups of foods? Water bath canners are used for acidic food, while pressure canners work for non-acidic food. Whether a food is acidic or not is reliant on its pH levels. Acidic food such as fruit have lower pH levels while meat and vegetables have alkaline or neutral levels. Both acidic and non-acidic food can kill dangerous bacteria at the temperature of a water bath canner, but *Botulinum* spores survive this process. Acidic food naturally kills these spores however, non-acidic food cannot and so a pressure canner is required for extra protection.

Some vegetables can be canned using the water bath method without the fear of *Botulinum spores*. *Botulinum* spores can be killed by lowering the pH level of the vegetables and making them more acidic. These low or extreme pH levels can be achieved by pickling the vegetables. To pickle the vegetables, simply submerge them in vinegar and that will make them more acidic. It should be acknowledged that this process will change the texture and taste of the vegetables. Meats and broth can only ever be safely processed through a pressure canner.

Which Brand Is Best?

When it comes to pressure canners, there are two brands that dominate the market, and with any good feud between two retail juggernauts comes the inevitable question. Which brand is best? Pepsi or Coke, Apple or Android, All-American or Presto? The answer is whatever you prefer. Apologies for this unsatisfactory answer, but both All-American and Presto pressure canners have their pros and cons. Ultimately, it is the customer's decision on what model makes them feel most comfortable. For first time pressure canner owners it is important to know what you're looking for and what brand is best for you.

All-American pressure canners come in a variety of sizes, which is perfect for people who plan on making large batches at a time. Their largest size will can 19 quart jars at a time, while their smallest holds only four. With this variety of sizes comes a variety of prices. Be prepared to spend more money for larger canners. All-American canners should only be used on a gas range instead of an electric one, so there is no stove damage. A feature of the All-American that makes them more user friendly is their weighted gauge. Instead of having to manually adjust the heat, weight on the valve regulates the pressure.

Presto pressure canners only come in two sizes which are the 16 quart liquid capacity model, and the 23 quart liquid capacity model. The Presto brand canners work with both gas and electric ranges. This fact, along with their small size, makes Presto more versatile than the All-American canners. The gauge is a dial gauge instead of a weighted one, and the pressure must be manually handled. This is better for people who wish to can in higher altitudes. Newer models have a button feature that drops down to inform you when the canner is safe to open.

As far as price goes, the Presto brand runs cheaper, and is more commonly available in stores such as Walmart. Presto canners do require the additional expense of replacing the rubber gasket around the inside of the lid. Gasket replacements are not very expensive however, and are only needed every few years. Keep in mind location when choosing between the two brands as well. High altitude places will prefer the presto while lower altitudes can enjoy the weighted gauge feature of the All-American. The decision between the two is also dependent on batch sizes. Investing in a larger All-American pressure canner will be the smarter option for those who have a good amount of canning orders to do in a short time. Presto canners are better for casual canning. Both brands are well built and last a long time.

Just because All-American and Presto are the most well known brands on the market, does not mean they are the only brands. Mirro, while not as popular, is the only brand other than the two aforementioned brands that is most recognized by professionals in the field of canning. Mirro, like Presto, only comes in two sizes: Both of these sizes have weighted gauge features like All-American canners. Fagor was another common brand until it was discontinued in 2018.

Does Size Matter?

When buying a pressure canner it's very important to choose a size that is going to work best for your canning experience. Size does matter: Different canning projects are going to require different size models. Is this a business opportunity, or do you just want to feed your family fresh carrots in the winter? It is also important to keep in mind when you're not using your pressure canner. Do you have the space for the biggest All-American model or would a smaller Presto fit in the cupboard better? These are just a few things to keep in mind before choosing a size of pressure canner.

To be considered a pressure canner by the USDA, the pot must be able to hold at least four quart jars. Presto and Mirro pressure canners start at an internal total volume of 16 quarts and those are the most commonly considered smallest canners. The smallest All-American model however, holds an internal total of 10 quarts. That does not mean the All-American model isn't a pressure canner though, because they do follow the USDA rule of being able to hold 4 quart jars. Anything smaller than this is considered a cooker and is not approved for canning by the USDA.

The University of Wisconsin Extension Service suggests only using a 16-22 quart pressure canner and believes anything less to be unsafe. All-American has two pressure canners under this limit at 10 and 15.5 quarts. It is essential to understand that All-American does not recommend using their canners under 16 quarts for smoked fish, as they do not have suitable processing times. Considering that both the Mirro and All-American brands make canners larger than 22 quarts, this is a strange limitation to put on the max volume of a pressure canner. In fact, using a pressure canner that is bigger than is required is not actually going to cause any danger.

Both Presto and Mirro start at 16 quarts although this size does have its limitations. The 16 quart models of each brand are just as wide as the 22 and 23 quart canners, but they lack their counterpart's height. Their smaller size slows down the canning process since you can not stack a second layer of half liter jars. Larger canners can also be used for water bath canning, but there just isn't room for this process in a 16 quart pressure canner. Their cons are outweighed by the fact that they do heat up and cool down faster than the larger canners.

Despite there being no safety issue in using a larger pressure canner for a smaller job, that doesn't mean bigger is always better. Keep in mind how efficiently you are using energy. Using a bigger pressure canner will increase your energy cost per jar, and considering one of the main goals of canning is to lower the cost of living, this is something to avoid. Remember that a bigger canner will also increase your carbon footprint, so if you plan on canning a lot, you might want to think about purchasing two canners in different sizes.

Other Considerations

Even if you know what brand and size you are looking for, there is still a lot to consider when buying a pressure canner. Most importantly how much they cost: Price varies on size and brand, but pressure canners range anywhere from 100 to 600 USD. Presto will usually be cheaper than Mirro or All-American, since it is more widely available. While pressure canners are a smart investment, it can be daunting to spend this much money on what could be considered a seasonal appliance. Mirro, Presto, and All-American are all very durable brands with available replacement parts, which makes buying a pressure canner second hand no problem. Just make sure to double check everything is in working condition or easily fixable before purchasing using this cheaper option.

Once again, make sure you have a distinct idea of what you're canning for before you purchase anything. If you are starting a home canned goods business, you are going to need a large and dependable pressure canner. A 600 dollar, 41 quart canner is a good idea because you can make the money back and the investment will pay off quicker. If you just want to can peas from your personal garden once a year, a smaller and cheaper model will do just as well. You should do what makes the most sense for your canning lifestyle.

Not everyone is able bodied, and unfortunately not all pressure canners are created with this in mind. The weight of the model you choose is very important. Since they are built to withstand pressure and hold jars, racks, and water, they are very heavy. The bigger the canner, the heavier it gets. Knowing your physical ability will help you choose a model that you can use with little to no issues. Your stove top should also be a factor in your model's weight. Large canners can easily crack a glass stove top. You don't want to ruin your kitchen before you have even had the chance to start canning.

Luckily, most pressure canners come with sets, but if you are buying second hand, sometimes you won't have everything you'll need. The following utensils are a mandatory investment every canner needs. Pressure canners always come with their own racks that sit at the bottom of the pot and hold the jars. You will also need jars as the whole point of pressure canning is to put food in jars. Another must have are canning tongs or jar lifters which will help to remove the jar from the rack when the pressure canner is finished cooling down. There are many kits available online with a variety of utensils that will make the process of canning much easier.

Even with all this information, choosing a pressure canner may still be an intimidating task, so here are some of my recommendations: If you are a beginner and only want to dabble in canning, I suggest a 16 quart Presto model. If you've been canning for a while and want to feed your family through the winter, either 22 quart Presto, 23 quart Mirro, or even a 25 quart All-American should work depending on the size of your family. If you have a year round canning business, a 30 or 41 quart All-American model is a good investment.

Chapter 2:

The Parts of a Pressure Canner

Gasket

A gasket is a rubber ring around the rim of the pressure canner lid. Its purpose is to seal in the contents and allow the canister to pressurize. It does this by stopping the steam from leaving the top of the kettle. Depending on your brand and model, gaskets are a very important feature and should be well taken care of. After every use, they need to be removed from the lid and thoroughly cleaned. Not only will this keep them in better condition for a longer time, but it will also sterilize the surface and stop the spread of any possible bacteria.

With time, the gasket becomes worn, and it is important to watch out for the rubber hardening or stretching. When this happens the gasket needs to be replaced to prevent any possible accidents. The recommended time in which to replace the gasket is anywhere between one and five years. Anything more than five years is often seen as pushing the gasket to its limit and unsafe in the canning community. The NCHFP says that you should wait no more than two years in between replacements. It also depends on how often the pressure canner is being used. Canners that often take on larger loads should have new gaskets every year.

While the brands Presto and Mirro require rubber gaskets to function, not all pressure canners use this part in their product. All-American pressure canners are the only brand to not have gaskets at all and instead seal metal to metal. The absence of the gasket doesn't make it any less safe however, and the metal to metal seal is more user friendly making the lid easier to open and close. While the other brands may have the minor inconvenience of replacing the gasket every few years, the price of said replacement is by no means a financial burden. On Amazon, a pack of rubber gaskets is available for under ten dollars.

With the need to replace the gasket every few years, you may feel tempted to stock up on them. Preparedness is often a virtue, but not necessarily in this case. Rubber gaskets are made from a fragile material, and even when they are not being used they are still subject to natural erosion. The verdict on how long you should keep a spare gasket or if you should even keep one at all is undecided. Some sources say they can last up to five years as long as they are kept in a cool and dry area. The brand Presto recommends buying them fresh and not using stored gaskets.

Your pressure canner will likely never explode; However, if it does, you might want to check the state of your gasket. It is widely considered the whole system's weakest link. Back in the days of old, before safety precautions were put in place, regulators would become clogged and place extreme pressure on these gaskets. The rubber gasket could not withstand these conditions for very long and would snap during the canning process. Pair this with the malfunction of a lid latch and thus the origin for the horror stories of flying pressure canner lids is born. Something like this happening today is very unlikely.

Weighted Gauge vs. Dial Gauge

A pressure gauge is supposed to monitor and help regulate pressure inside of the canner. There are three different models of gauges that you can find on a pressure canner. The first and oldest is a dial gauge that is used to measure the pressure within the pot. The downside to this is that it can't control the pressure. A weighted gauge is the opposite: It controls the pressure but can't measure it. Lastly is a dual-gauge, which is a hybrid of the two. It has a dial for reading the pressure levels, but also utilizes weight to regulate that pressure.

A dial gauge has a watch face design that is used to display numbers relating to the amount of pressure being applied. Since a dial gauge can't control the amount of pressure in the pot, it requires a more hands on approach. You need to adjust the burner heat to change the pressure. This is helpful for higher altitudes because they require different pressure to properly process. It is possible for dial gauges to become inaccurate with age or if they are bumped around. In consideration of safety, it is fine if the food is cooked with too high of pressure, but the quality will be lackluster.

Dial gauges need to be checked at least once a year. This is generally carried out at the start of canning season, after the pressure canner is taken out of storage. This can be done by taking it to your local extension service. If you don't have a local extension service it will be unwise to invest in this type of gauge. You can also do it yourself if you have the dual-gauge feature. If the gauge is off by more than two when tested at 11 pounds then it should be replaced. Anything under is fine as long as you adjust to the difference with the heater when you are cooking. Also, if the glass on a dial gauge breaks or goes missing, it's time to get a new one.

If a dial gauge is manual, then a weighted gauge can be considered an automatic regulator. There are three settings of weights for this gauge and they are 5, 10, and 15. When the pound per square inch or PSI is reached this gauge will signal this by jiggling and making a rattling noise. Despite the fact that weighted gauges come in 5, and 10, the desired pressure is actually slightly over that. They are at this weight because weighted gauges don't release at exactly this PSI. That's why recipes are different for dial gauges and read to release pressure at 6 and 11 pounds.

The dual-gauge is just using both methods. Since weighted gauges are less hands on, the dial gauge is mostly there to keep track of where the PSI is at. It can be a back up if something goes wrong, but to be honest, it is kind of useless. Modern Presto canners are mostly dial gauge, but they've made their pot compatible with dual-gauges. The weights are sold separately. This is helpful for people who prefer the dial gauge way, but aren't close enough to a local extension service to get their dial checked every year.

Vent Pipe

The vent pipe is located on the lid of your pressure canner. It is a small opening where steam and pressure are vented out from the pot during the canning process. This is where the weighted gauge is placed. It will jiggle on top of the vent pipe when the weight is reached, making a rattling sound. The vent blows out steam automatically when the pressure attained is above 15 PSI. The vent pipe is one of the most important pieces and the pressure canner should never be used if this is damaged in any sort of way.

To clean the vent pipe, you will need a pipe cleaner or a string to pull through the vent opening. This piece is harder to clean, but it doesn't require you to remove it from the lid. Make sure not to use too much soap or other cleaning supplies that can dry and clog the vent. Don't try to clean the vent pipe with a toothpick or anything similar, as it can break and become lodged inside. Before using the canner, it is always smart to check if anything is clogging the vent pipe. To do this, hold the lid up to a light source so it is easier to see inside.

If the vent pipe is bent or damaged, you will need to replace it. You can also replace it if the inside has become corroded with rust or other foreign objects. Every pressure canner is different and so the method of removing the vent pipe will vary. No matter the brand, you will need a wrench to unscrew it from the lid. If it is stuck, you can use olive oil as lubricant. Make sure to wash your new vent pipe before you screw it in. It should be a relatively easy replacement that your owner's manual can help with. New vent pipes aren't expensive either, so there's no need to worry about putting a hole in your pocket.

There are some problems to look out for when it comes to the vent pipe's functions. Modern pressure canners have an overpressure plug that releases when the vent pipe fails, so there's no reason to be afraid if something goes wrong. You might be alarmed if condensation starts to appear under the regulator. This is normal because the pressure regulator starts off at a lower temperature than the lid. If it continues it could loosen the vent pipe, though. If you notice a lot of moisture during a process, feel free to tighten the vent pipe back up with a wrench once it is finished.

Overpressure Plug

The overpressure plug is a small, black piece of rubber that acts as a safety precaution when the vent pipe fails. When the overpressure plug is new it should be soft and pliable. This is important for its function, so make sure to replace brittle overpressure plugs as soon as you can. If the vent pipe becomes obstructed, the overpressure plug pops out of its hole on the lid and allows for the steam to exit the canner. This is the only safe way to release pressure when the vent pipe is no longer doing its job. When the canning process begins, it is normal to see a small amount of steam leaking from the area around the plug. This will stop once it seals.

To clean or replace the overpressure plug, you are going to need to pop it out of the opening on the lid. It should be fairly easy to do with a gentle push. To put the plug back in it's spot, flip the lid so the inside is facing you. The domed side of the plug should go first into the hole from this side. Push it in until it is even against the lid. If it isn't sealed right, steam will leak and ruin the PSI of the canning process. Some overpressure plugs will read TOP on the dome side. This should be visible from the top side of the lid.

Before each use of your canner, you will want to double check that the overpressure plug is still in good condition and capable of sealing in the pressure. It will also need to be cleaned in between loads. Since the plugs are made out of rubber like gaskets are, they are susceptible to the same problems. They can dry out quicker if they are regularly washed. Make sure to dry them off completely before putting them back in because you don't want the hole to rust over. Keep them away from direct exposure to high heat as well. A stovetop could easily melt the rubber and make them deteriorate faster.

Overpressure plugs need to be replaced at least every three years. Most canners suggest replacing them when you are replacing the gasket because both parts are made from rubber that cracks and deforms at the same pace. They need to be replaced as soon as they start to deform. Overpressure plugs are the last line of defense. If they are not in the condition they need to be, the canner could explode from too much pressure and no release. Replacements are easy to get and available for a decent price online.

Canning Rack

When you buy a pressure canner, it will usually come with a canning rack. If you have purchased yours second hand or your model just didn't come with one, you will want to invest in a canning rack. They sit at the bottom of the pot and hold the jars during the canning process. Jars can not touch any side of the pot or else they will not evenly heat up. This guarantees heat circulation and evenly canned food. It also keeps the jars from touching each other. The last thing you want is for your jars to break or chip during the process which can happen if they are not evenly dispersed.

It is common for canners to double deck within a load. This means having two rows of jars on top of each other. The National Center for Home Food Preservation has okayed double decking for both pressure canning and water bath canning. You can use a second rack for this, but it isn't necessary as long as the jars are staggered for weight distribution. There are special racks made for double decking to make it easier for certain size jars. Double decking does not change the amount of water to put in the pot or how long it takes to can.

Just like any canning equipment, remember to wash it after every use and then thoroughly dry it to prevent rust. Like the pressure canner, you can use steel wool to get stubborn stains off. Unless it is made from a non-metal, then you should use a more appropriate cleaning method. When it is time to store the canning rack, keep it in a dry area away from the humidity. You can wrap it in a paper towel to keep the dust off of it. If you have a metal canning rack, they will likely rust eventually and have to be replaced.

There are several different types of canning racks: The most popular are the ones made from stainless steel. These will last a very long time and come in a variety of different sizes that will suit your canner's model. There is also the aluminum canning rack that is similar to the stainless steel one. They are just as common and durable, and happen to be the cheaper option. If you want to avoid rust, you can buy a plastic rack. The downside to this option is that they aren't as durable, which is probably why they're not as common as their metal counterparts. Lastly, there are silicone racks. These are easy to clean like the plastic rack and can be used in pressure cookers too.

Whichever type of canning rack you get, make sure you fit it to the size of your model. This will just be simpler if you buy a canner that already comes with a rack. They are easy to buy though, so you don't have to worry if it's not the most financially beneficial decision for you. If you're overwhelmed by all the choices, I will suggest buying an aluminum pressure rack. It is just as durable and reliable as stainless steel but for a cheaper price. Some people don't buy canning racks at all and get very creative with DIY racks. If you'd rather research ways to do that, it is safe as long as it doesn't fall apart.

Chapter 3:

Pressure Canning Preparation

Choosing a Recipe

Choosing a recipe should be the easiest part of using a pressure canner, right? Just use one of your grandmother's old recipes that have been passed down for generations. If it worked for your ancestors then it should work for you. Unless it doesn't and you're unlucky enough to contract botulism. The truth about using an old family recipe is that you don't actually know what safety protocols whoever wrote it was following. That doesn't necessarily mean that you have to give up on generations of canning traditions. Just make sure it aligns with the USDA's canning guidelines. It's always better to change your dear, old, departed Grandma's recipe than to join her.

Not everyone comes from a long line of canning ancestors. First generation canners have to rely on their own resources to find suitable recipes. Thankfully we live in the age of the internet and a safe and tasty meal is only a few clicks away. With a boatload of information comes a boatload of confusion however, so be careful choosing a recipe online. Only use recipes that are specific to pressure canners. The two methods of canning, the water bath method and the pressure can method, require different treatments and preparation for the jar's contents and should not be used interchangeably.

You should also only choose recipes that are on or below your level of expertise. There are plenty of available canning recipes for beginners online or at your local library. If you aren't comfortable with the recipe you may become distracted, which is the last thing you want to be when operating heavy equipment such as the pressure canner. It is best to start with simpler recipes and work your way up to more complicated ones. This rule applies to new canners as well. If you aren't comfortable with your new model, don't start off with an expert level recipe even if you have years of experience.

While the internet can be a wonderful place for new canners to find and share delicious recipes, this is not always the case. Not everyone on the internet is a pressure canning scholar, even if they claim to be one. Always make sure the recipe you choose comes from a reliable source. In this case, a reliable source refers to any recipe that aligns with the guidelines from the USDA. I suggest reading through these guidelines before choosing a recipe, so you know what to look out for. It is best to further research specific recipes if you are uncertain if they follow these guidelines.

Lastly, pick a recipe that is actually achievable for your appliance and supplies. If you're using a recipe that calls for fresh meat, but all you have is frozen chicken breasts from the grocery store, then maybe look for a recipe that fits your ingredients better. You don't want to be overzealous with your canning either, especially if you have an older pressure canner. You certainly don't want to overwhelm the machine and accidentally send it into an early retirement because you wanted 300 jars of fresh peas. It also helps to know how many jars and lids you'll need so there won't be any potential extra waste.

Preparing the Food

Before you even touch the pressure canner, your first job is to make sure that the food is ready to be canned. Different food requires different preparation, so make sure to thoroughly research your meal before you start. Have a clean preparation area, as cross contamination can lead to bacteria growth. This is especially vital if you plan on canning more than one type of meat. It is important to know the pH levels of what you are canning as well. You could pressure can acidic food with little to no problem, but it is unnecessary since a water bath canner is perfectly safe.

Most canning resources are going to recommend the freshest of ingredients. Do you have to follow this advice? Technically no, but the fresher the food the better the taste. It also has a longer shelf life than over-processed food does. Fresher food has more health benefits as well, so I have to highly recommend following this advice. Remember to carefully examine your vegetables before canning, as you don't want bruised or potentially rotting food. If you discover a brown spot or some kind of lesion, you don't have to throw away the whole piece, just cut off the bad part.

Prior to placing the food into jars, you should know whether you want to cold pack or hot pack. Cold pack is often referred to as raw pack and is the process of putting unheated food into the jars. The jars still need to be warm though, so whatever syrup, water, or juice you add should be boiled beforehand. Hot packing is the process of using freshly boiled food. Before adding hot packed food to the jars, let it simmer for a few minutes. The syrup, water, or juice added to the hot pack still needs to be boiled, as well.

Raw packing is mostly used for pressure canning, while hot packing is best for the water bath method. This is because hot packing is the superior way to get rid of any air within the food tissues by boiling it first. Food contains 10-30% more air before it is canned, but this air would cause discoloration quickly within the jars. Raw packing only lasts about two to three month in storage before they become discolored. This is unfortunate but also the only safe way to can non-acidic foods. Hot packing also shrinks the food which allows for more room in the jars.

It is suggested to start to can your prepared food as soon as possible. With unnecessary exposure to air comes the browning, bruising, and ultimate loss of flavor that we are looking to avoid. With fruits, you should always keep your cut up pieces in a water-diluted ascorbic acid bath. This will help to keep them fresh and acidic. Vegetables don't require this however, as they are not acidic, and are canned in pressure canners only. Non-acidic food such as meat and vegetables still need to be protected from oxygen and other enzymes, and therefore should be rushed for maximum freshness.

Jar Preparation

Despite its name, pressure canning isn't putting food into cans. This is probably because the word jarring isn't very aesthetic, with its negative connotations of being shocked or disturbed. The act of putting food into jars is relaxing and positive, so it needs a name that aligns with its values. Even though it's called canning, do not put aluminum cans in a pressure canner: It won't work and it's not safe. Some people have used steel cans, but it's a complicated process and there isn't that much reading material available for it. Pressure canning, especially for beginners, should only ever be done with jars

Remember that not all jars work in pressure canners. Since pressure canners reach higher temperatures than water bath canners, not all jars are compatible with both methods. The mason jar brand Ball is most widely approved for pressure canning use. Commercial jars, like for spaghetti sauce that you can find at the grocery, should not be used in a pressure canner: These are one use jars. The lids are usually one piece and aren't safe for a second use, while the glass isn't made to withstand the heat. They also don't come in the same sizes as mason jars and will not fit into the canner the same way.

Mason jars usually last around ten years. Anything more than that and you might face chipping issues. While antique jars may look pretty and are in good condition, it is not safe to use them in a pressure canner. Most jars that are from the 70's or earlier aren't made out of tempered glass and can't survive the temperatures inside of a pressure canner. If a jar cracks inside of the pressure canner, the product within it cannot be used, and so investing in new jars is always the better option. Mason jars are usually available in bulk for a reasonable price.

Always clean your jars before and after use. You don't want any dust or debris clinging to the sides of your jar ready to contaminate your food. Hot water and white vinegar is great for getting rid of any unwanted, filmy residue. You can also just run it through the dishwasher. Watch out for soapy jars because it will make your food taste like soap. After you have finished cleaning, the jars need to be sanitized: Which is not the same thing. The sanitizing step can be skipped if the food's pressure canning process takes more than 10 minutes. Sanitizing is just boiling the jars in water for 10 minutes. Make sure to remove the jars with tongs when they are done sanitizing so you don't accidentally burn yourself.

The jar lids should still be cleaned as well, but they don't need to be sanitized. Mason jar lids come in two parts: The screw band and the lid. The lid is made from metal and rubber and comes into direct contact with the food. That is why they need to be thrown out and replaced after one use. The metal screw bands are reusable and can be washed with warm water and dish soap. They do need to be completely dried however, as a wet screw band could affect the seal and allow bacteria to get in. Keeping them dry will also prevent rust.

Familiarize Yourself With Your Model

Pressure canners are not the type of thing to just jump into the deep end with. While modern canners are very safe, there is the very small chance of something unfortunate happening. That's why it is vital for you to familiarize yourself with your pressure canner before you start using it. If your canner is brand new, it will come with written directions: This will be your holy scripture. Read it, preach it, live by it. If your pressure canner is second hand and it doesn't come with directions, you can likely find instructions for it online as long as you know the brand and model.

Understanding your model's size capacity is often overlooked. The instructions should say how many jars will fit inside your canner. If for some reason it doesn't, don't make a guess and go with it. Look it up online by your pressure canner's brand and model. Jars will usually be described in the sizes of quarts or pints. Only use these size jars as anything else hasn't been approved upon by your brand for that model. Never over stuff your pressure canner or it could result in broken glass. The only thing worse than hot steam going everywhere is hot steam *and* glass.

No matter what brand you choose, all models are different. As long as your pressure canner isn't from the 1950's, you should have a thoroughly enjoyable experience using your model. To ensure this, you need to know how all of its pieces work. Some models have gaskets, while some don't and close metal to metal. Brands have different moving pieces like, for instance, All-American are weighted gauge canners while Presto is available in dial gauge styles. These require different approaches and should not be treated as the same thing. Not every recipe is going to take this into account, and that is why reading your directions is so crucial. Know your model and how it works.

Knowing your model also requires you to know the utensils that come with it. Canning utensil kits usually come with more things than you'll know what to do with. Don't waste space in your kitchen, learn how to utilize all these tools. Whether it is a tong or a jar wrench, your canning experience will be so much easier. If your pressure canner didn't come with a kit because it's second hand or it just wasn't part of the deal, investing in one will be a smart idea. Kits save so much time and prevent possible accidents.

The most important part of knowing your pressure canner is knowing when the process is done. Recipes will tell you how long a specific food will take, but you will still have to wait until the depressuring is finished. With most models, the dial gauge will read zero and that's when you'll know the pot is safe to open. This isn't always the case, though, and that's why reading your owner's manual will help you avoid any mistakes. Some newer pressure canners have features that lock the lid until the pot is fully depressurized. It is possible that an older model pressure canner doesn't even have a gauge and you will have to time it yourself.

Test Run

The exact process for a test run is explained in Chapter 4, where we will go over how to actually use your pressure canner. These are just tips to pull off your test run as smoothly as possible. Now you may be thinking, "Do I even need a test run? How complicated can this even be?" Pressure canners aren't actually that complicated at all, but they can be if you don't know what you are doing. That's why a test run is the perfect place to find your footing and to become comfortable with your equipment before starting on larger, more complicated loads.

Before your test run, go through your chosen recipe again. Read it as many times as it takes to fully understand what it is telling you. Cooking times and the amount of pressure applied are not recommendations. They are the difference between safe and deadly. Hopefully the recipe you choose has been tested time and time again for optimal taste as well. The recipe will also give you tips on whether to hot pack or raw pack the food. Pay close attention to this because it affects the preparation for the water that goes in the pressure canner before you start cooking.

You should also start small for your test run. Adapt the recipe or choose a different one that requires a smaller amount of jars. Hot packing recipes don't use as much due to shrinkage, but they do take a little more prep time. If you start with a smaller amount of jars, it will be easier to focus on the pressure canning itself. If you have a large canner, don't worry about utilizing all the space. Fewer jars won't change the outcome and it will still be safe to eat. Don't make this a habit though as it is a waste of energy.

A test run should be done with an easy product to can. The food that I highly suggest starting off with is green beans. Green beans are very versatile when it comes to planning meals. They are the perfect side to nearly any entree. It is also one of the most simple vegetables to pressure can. You have the option to either hot pack or cold pack green beans. Since the minimum is only two quart jars at a time, you can hot pack them and not worry about a larger load. Corn and carrots are other great vegetables to start off with, however, you don't have to do your first test run with veggies. Meat and stock are not that much more complicated and are just as versatile.

Now that you've reread your recipe and know exactly what food and how much you're cooking, you are ready to start your test run. This may seem daunting, but it is highly unlikely anything will go wrong. The pressure canner is very safe as long as you are using it properly. Your main focus through your test run is paying attention. Pay attention to the gauge. Pay attention to the timer. Pay attention to your appliance as a whole. If anything does happen to go wrong, you will be way ahead of it as long as you've been paying attention.

Chapter 4:

How to Use a Pressure Canner

Preparing the Pressure Canner

After you've prepared everything else, it is time to prepare your canner. The first step is inspecting the pot. The pressure canner should never get dirty with food since it's in jars, but if it has just been taken out of storage it could be covered in dust. The pressure canner can be cleaned with hot, soapy water. Make sure to thoroughly rinse the soap off and then dry it. Don't forget to wash the lid and gasket, as well. After you check the canner for dust, make sure to check for any natural wear and tear. If you are uncertain about any corrosion, don't use it. It is better to be safe than sorry.

The canning rack will be the next thing to inspect. Even if you have just bought your pressure canner and canning rack, you should still give it a thorough cleaning as you don't know where it has been. The jar rack can be cleaned in the same way as the pot with hot and soapy water. If you are having trouble removing stains, using steel wool will work better than using a regular sponge. You will not want soapy steam, so make sure the rack is completely rinsed off. After it has dried, place it at the bottom of the pot.

You will then add water to the pressure canner. You do not want this water to have soap or any other strange particles in it: That is why everything is thoroughly rinsed out before it is used. In the water bath method, the pot is filled to cover all the jars, but a pressure canner uses less water. The goal of the pressure canner is to boil this water into hot steam. In most cases the water is two to three inches deep. Some pressure canners have different qualifications, though, so you should always double check the owner's manual.

Your jars should already be cleaned and if you prefer, sanitized. Follow your recipe and jar your ingredients in a timely manner to optimize freshness. Before putting on the lids, make sure there are no air bubbles that could possibly lead to food spoilage. You will want to wipe the rim of the jar after adding the food to make sure nothing can stop the jar from sealing. Place the lid flatly on the top of the jar and screw down the band. This should be tight enough that it will stay sealed, but not too tightly that it can't be opened again. When the jars have been securely tightened, place them gently at the bottom of the pot in the canning rack.

Before the canner can start pressurizing, you will need to close the lid. How this can be done will vary from brand to brand. If you have a Mirro or Presto brand, double check that your gasket is in good condition and ready to be used. If you are uncertain on how to close your lid, check the owner's manual. It is very important that the lid is fastened shut: The last thing you want is for the top to pop off in the middle of the canning process. Some models have mechanisms that close the lid until the canner is done depressurizing. If you have one of these models, make sure this feature is in working condition and has properly sealed the pot without any leaks.

Pressurizing

Congratulations, you have made it to the process of pressurization! Times vary when it comes to processing so it is important to pay attention to your recipe and follow it closely. Of particular consideration is your altitude. There are three steps to the pressurizing process which I refer to as vent, plug, and rattle. Before you begin, make sure you have whatever regulator your pressure canner uses nearby because you will need it. Also make sure you have some sort of timer so you don't accidentally over-process your canned goods. Remember to pay attention, too, as this is the most dangerous part to mess up at.

Finally after all the work of preparation, you can turn the pressure canner on. The heat needs to be turned on high. Give the canner a few minutes to warm up. Once it is hot enough, steam will start coming out of the vent pipe. You want this steam to be coming out in a steady stream. This is the start of the pressurizing process. Get a timer and set it to ten minutes because that is how long you should let the pressure canner vent. It is possible for steam to be present around the lid lock, which will pop up around when the pressure canner is done venting.

Next, you will place your regulator on top of the steam spout. If you have a weighted gauge regulator, make sure it is set at the right weight. The weight you should use will usually be specified in your recipe. Keep in mind, different altitudes have different requirements for the amount of weight you should put on it. Oftentimes, it is anywhere between 10 to 15 pounds of pressure. If you don't have a weighted gauge model just pay attention to your dial gauge. Be careful when you place the regulator on the steam spout as it can be very hot: Oven mitts will keep you safe from the heat.

The next step is more waiting: Eventually the regulator will start to rattle. It shouldn't take that much time for this to occur, though. Take out the timer again and set it to the recipe specified canning time. Once more, you should adjust the time to your altitude provisions, since that can affect processing times. Depending on your type of pressure canner, you may have to wait until the regulator starts to rock and then adjust the heat to achieve the stable rattling noise. If you have a dial-gauge canner, wait until the gauge reads 11 pounds to start timing.

If for any reason your pressure goes below the recommended amount, you need to bring the pressure back up and start the timer over again. This loss of pressure will result in unprocessed food. If you find the pressure going above the recommended amount, your jars may lose liquid. This will result in less full jars and possibly discoloration. **It is imperative that you do not open the pressure canner at any point in the pressurizing process.** The pot is full of boiling hot steam that can burn you or anyone else nearby. If this does happen, seek medical attention immediately.

Depressurizing

Don't open the lid just yet: Your pressure canner is still full of hot steam that has the potential to cause a serious burn. You have just completed the pressurization process, but that doesn't mean you are done just yet. The pressure canner needs time to cool down. This is the process of depressurizing where the steam is released in a safe way. Depressuring doesn't require as much care and attention as the process of pressurizing, but it is still very easy to get hurt. Have your oven mitt ready because the regulator and other parts of the pressure canner may still be hot.

The first step to depressurizing is to turn off the heat. From here the pot will slowly start to cool down. It is important that you don't try to rush this process in any way. If you try to force the pot to cool down, it could result in spoilage. Now, if you're wondering how one would even attempt this, there are two common ways people mess up the cooling process: One way is to use cool water on the canner. This has the capability to warp the shape of the pressure canner lid. The second way is opening the vent pipe before it is ready. This will mess with the sealing process and ruin the goods.

Depending on your model, there are different ways to know when the pressure canner is fully finished depressurizing. Some models have a safety valve that will drop down when the process is complete. Not all models are this convenient, though, and some have to rely on the dial gauge. The dial gauge will read zero pounds pressure after everything has cooled down. Dial gauges aren't always the most reliable, however, so proceed with caution. The time in which a pressure canner takes to cool down varies depending on how old the model is. Older models have thicker walls and take longer than the newer, thin-walled pressure canners. If your pressure canner doesn't have a dial gauge or a safety valve, you'll have to time it yourself. These are usually heavier models and take about 30 minutes to depressurize.

Now it is time to remove the pressure regulator. Even if the dial gauge is at zero, you should still use an oven mitt for this because steam will come out of the vent pipe. You should not remove the regulator if it is still rattling. If your dial gauge is at zero and it's still rattling, then you probably have a broken dial gauge. In that case, the jar's contents are not safe to eat and should be either reprocessed as soon as possible, or just thrown away. Don't open the lid as soon as the steam stops as this could still result in a possible accident. Wait 10 minutes from the time you removed the regulator for optimal safety.

The depressurizing process has finished and you can safely remove the lid from the pot. Since opening and closing the lid is different from model to model, consult your owner's manual if you are unsure on how to do this. After you unfasten the lid make sure to lift it in a way that protects yourself from any possible steam escaping the canister. You have succeeded so far and it would be a shame to end this positive experience with a burnt face. You also don't want to accidentally burn your hands so use your trusty oven mitt when handling the lid.

Removing the Contents

The last part of the canning process is removing the jars from the canner. Let's not get too ahead of ourselves yet though, because the pot is still very hot. The jars should be left in the pressure canner for at least ten minutes after the lid has been removed. This gives them enough time to cool slightly. The jars are still going to be way too hot to touch with your bare hand, but it will still be safe to remove them. Don't try to speed up the natural cooling time with cold water or you could accidentally break the jars.

When the ten minutes are up, use a jar lifter to remove the contents of the canner. Jar lifters or tongs come in canning kits and can be found online for a decent price. Do not use your hand. This should be done very carefully, so only lift one jar at a time; To the best of your ability try to avoid tilting the jar, as its seal is still fragile. The jars should be carefully placed on a kitchen towel or wire cooling rack, away from any cold draft. Placing the jars on a cold surface could lead to breakage. Leave about one inch of space in between the jars so they are not touching.

The jars should be left to cool for the next 12 to 24 hours. At no point before this time should the lids be tightened or touched. The sealing process is completely finished when the jars are entirely cooled. Once this time period has passed, test the seals by pressing on the lid. If it pops up or down something went wrong with the sealing. Just because the sealing failed doesn't mean the food has to be thrown out. You can refrigerate it but make sure it is consumed as soon as possible. Before you get ready to store the jars, take off the screw bands. They are no longer needed to keep the jar closed and you can reuse them for another time.

Date the lid of the jars with a permanent marker so you can know when they go bad. The lid will be discarded later, so you don't need to mark the jar's glass every time. It will also be helpful to label the jar with its ingredients just in case you forget later on. Most people store their canned goods in their basement but it doesn't matter where you put them as long as it is cool and dry. It is also important that it is out of direct sunlight as that can spoil the food faster. For optimal quality, canned goods should be used within one year. If the label on a canned good has disappeared, rubbed off, or is unreadable in any way, there is no safety risk but the contents might not taste as good.

After the jars have been removed from the pressure canner and it has cooled to a reasonable temperature, you can start washing it. Before and after use, the canner, lid, and gasket all need to be washed, rinsed, and dried. It is very important to completely dry these pieces to avoid mold and rust. The screw bands should also be washed before they are put in storage. Your owner's manual should have a complete guide to the safe storage of your pressure canner, but we'll go over it in Chapter 9 as well. Once clean up is finished, feel free to enjoy one of your delicious canned meals.

Common Errors and How to Fix Them

Even if you did everything perfectly according to the recipe, the owner's manual and the USDA guidelines, mistakes can still happen. Not everything is your control and that's okay because most errors can be fixed. Pressure canners have a lot of moving parts that need constant upkeep. If one thing goes under the radar, the whole process can be messed up. Not everything can be checked before you start pressure canning and by the time you realize something is wrong, it can be too late to save the food. This is unfortunate, but it is also not always the outcome.

One of the worst things that can happen is an inaccurate dial gauge. If you realize that your dial gauge is off by a couple pounds then it's time to get a replacement. Don't trust food that was canned with an inaccurate dial gauge. If it's over-processed it is going to be inedible, but if it's under-processed it could be contaminated with dangerous bacteria. Dial gauges should be checked for accuracy at least once a year. This can be done by going to your local county extension service. If it is off by under two pounds, it can still be used just make sure to consciously adjust it.

Another side effect of the natural wear and tear of moving parts is having a stuck lid. Even after everything has cooled and your pressure canner is safe to open, it won't open. This is a rubber gasket problem: When gaskets get old they start to harden making the lid more difficult to open. Lubricant can be a temporary fix, but it is time to get a new gasket. They are available online for a reasonable price. If you really need to use your pressure canner and can't wait until the replacement comes in, you can rub the gasket with olive oil and it shouldn't stick anymore. To get the lid unstuck, tap it gently with a hammer and repeat every few minutes until it comes off.

Sometimes when removing the jars you might notice some air bubbles floating to the top. This doesn't mean your food hasn't been processed correctly or that something went wrong with sealing. It is actually quite common and there is no reason to be upset. Air bubbles are normal to see up to after two hours post pressure canning. You should only start to worry when it's been a couple days and there are still air bubbles. At that point, the food is probably fermenting and should be thrown out. It is likely that something did go wrong with the sealing process so you might want to check the jar for cracks.

Another common problem people find when they remove the jars from the canner, is a loss of liquid. You filled up the jars to the recommended spot, and yet now they look less full. Once again this is a normal occurrence and is called siphoning. There's no reason to be alarmed unless the jar is less than half full of liquid. If this is the problem then something did go wrong and the jar is probably not sealed. Always check the lid after the jars have cooled even if the jars are more than half full. If the jar hasn't sealed, make sure to refrigerate the contents.

Chapter 5:

What Can Can and What Can't Can

When to Use a Pressure Canner

As previously discussed there are two methods to canning. The water bath method uses boiling water to heat and seal in the food while the pressure canner uses steam. The water bath method can be used in any large enough pot while pressure canning can't be safely performed without an actual pressure canner. A pressure canner can heat to 240 degrees Fahrenheit. This is around 30 degrees higher than the capacities of a water bath canner that only reaches temperatures of 212 degrees Fahrenheit. These are the only two recommended ways to can food. Under no circumstance should a pressure cooker be used to can food as they are not big enough.

When it comes to the decision on whether to use a pressure canner or a water bath, it is not really up to you. It all depends on the acidic level of your food. Acidic cuisine doesn't require high temperatures and can kill off bacteria all on its own. Non-acidic food has to be processed in a pressure canner or it has the possibility of becoming contaminated with deadly bacteria. How can you tell if a food is acidic? Well you could guess, but that is not very safe. Good thing this chapter will provide a comprehensive list of what can can and what can't can in a pressure canner.

Water bath canners are primarily used for fruit and fruit products. Fruit is acidic and does not require a pressure canner for safe consumption. The same goes for other acidic food such as salsa, pickles, and relish. Vegetables, on the other hand, should not be eaten unless they are canned in a pressure canner. Meat and stews should also only be processed with a pressure canner. Not all fruit is ready for a water bath straight from harvest. For instance, figs are considered to be low-acid fruits but as long as you add a little bit of lemon juice to your concoction, a water bath canner will be fine.

The age-old question is finally answered when it comes to deciding on a canning method. Is a tomato a fruit a vegetable? Technically, scientists have already decided that it is fruit. Seeing as the tomato can safely be processed in a water bath canner, the canning community must concur. Since they are so multifaceted when it comes to meal planning, tomatoes are a popular choice for many canners. They are very acidic to start off with but oftentimes, for extra safety, lemon juice is added to the jars to make them process better in the water bath.

You don't need to pressure can fruit but there isn't really danger to it. The worst case scenario is that the fruit doesn't taste as good as it could have. There is a serious danger to water bath canning vegetables or meat though. There is a way to change the acid levels in vegetables if you really want to use a water bath canner. Pickling the veggies is a common way canners bypass this rule. This can be done by fermenting them in a bath of vinegar. It is not recommended to pickle meat as an attempt to water bath can it.

Vegetable Do's and Don'ts

Many vegetables come out of a pressure canner delicious and ready to eat. This will not always happen though. It is important to listen to your recipe because different vegetables need to be prepared in different ways. There are several things to account for before you start canning. Vegetables are non-acidic and you will have to use a pressure canner with them if they are not pickled. That doesn't mean starch levels and amount of nutrients is the same across the board. Flavor, health, and even the shape or form of the vegetable should be considered before you pick a recipe.

There are some vegetables that are favorites to can among canners and they are green beans, carrots, and corn. They make for the best side dishes and are very versatile when it comes to choosing a recipe. They are also very cheap and easy to experiment with when you are first starting your canning journey. Carrots are some of the healthiest vegetables packed full with important dietary vitamins. If you are interested in the health benefits of carrots make sure to find a recipe that doesn't add unnecessary starch. Corn, in addition to some other favorite veggies like potatoes and peas, are very starchy. This means they are healthy in moderation only. Potatoes are usually hot packed to limit the amount of starch seeping into the jar during processing.

Spinach has been found to be one of, if not, the healthiest vegetable. Not only are they full of vitamins, but they are also enriched with antioxidants that fight off cancer and other chronic diseases. Beets are another wonderful choice, but they have a flavor that works better for a more mature pallet. Peppers make a great addition to any salad and sauce. Asparagus is another powerhouse of health and provides a delicious flavor for fewer calories. There are many, many other vegetables that work wonders in a pressure canner but that doesn't mean all do.

All vegetables can be safely processed in a pressure canner but that doesn't mean they are going to taste good. Any and all pressure canned vegetables will not pose any risk to your health as long as the process is done correctly. Most problems arise from the vegetables that are naturally soft. Squash is not a good choice for a pressure canner despite their healthy nature. They can be pickled but a pressure canner's high heat will not work well with the squash's texture that will become edible mush. More vegetables that are subject to mush are cauliflower, broccoli, eggplant, artichoke, and olives. These will do better being pickled and then being processed with the lower heat of a water bath canner. The only time cabbage should be canned using any method is as sauerkraut in a water bath canner. Lettuce should only be eaten fresh as any attempt to preserve the veggie will result in sub-par flavor.

Meat Do's and Don'ts

Meat Do's and Don'ts are pretty simple. You can can anything that isn't rotten meat. All meats are not created equal however, and will require different processing times and PSI. Always double check the recipes because one little mess up can cause contamination. Botulism is more common in vegetables, but that doesn't make meat immune so it is important to only ever use a pressure canner. Meat can not be pickled to use in a water bath canner like veggies can. According to the USDA, there is no safe way to raise the acidic level of any kind of meat.

Does it matter if the meat isn't fresh? Well, it won't change whether or not the meat can be canned in a pressure canner. Frozen meat can still be canned as long as it is still good to eat. Most recipes are going to call for farm fresh meat, though. This is because it will taste better. Food that is frozen loses its flavor quickly. If you don't have the stomach to supply fresh meat yourself, don't worry. Local butchers shops are always the best bet for fresh beef and poultry. Most supermarkets have a deli counter as well. If you live by a body of water, you could find a nearby fishmonger.

If you enjoy hunting, canning is a great way to keep your big game safe to eat for longer. A large buck can easily last you a year if it is canned properly. You should always find a recipe that matches whatever you bring home. A recipe for venison will not work for rabbit meat. Hunting and canning have often come hand and hand so many animals that you can legally hunt have a readily available recipe. As long as you have a license to hunt it, then there's no limit to what you can't can. However, good luck finding enough shelf space for a full-sized black bear.

If you have a vegetarian or vegan lifestyle, you might be wondering what meat alternatives can be canned. This is all dependent on what the meat alternatives are made from. While many alternatives are advertised as plant-based, they can also include ingredients that won't work in any method. The brand Beyond Meat has most of their available food marketed as plant-based, but this isn't just vegetables and includes grains. Grains cannot be processed in a canner and shouldn't be used as an ingredient for a canning recipe. Anything that includes soy, will also not work. Which means tofu and Impossible burgers can't be canned either.

Other Foods You Can Can

Pressure canning isn't just for meats and vegetables. It is for canning anything that is non-acidic and can't fight off the *Botulinum* bacteria itself. The only other group of food that really falls into this category is soups and stocks. Most soups are made with meat or vegetable products anyway, and so they have much of the same principles when it comes to canning. Make sure to follow a tested and trusted recipe since soups often have a mixture of ingredients. Meat and vegetables don't usually have the same processing times or PSI, but when they are together in soup they have to. Don't be your own guinea pig, let someone else find the middle ground for this.

Some things, as we will go over in the next section, should never be canned in a pressure canner. Do not use these in your soups or stocks. These ingredients can always be added in later when you are ready to eat the food. Not only is it potentially dangerous, but it's also just going to ruin the flavor. This means some of your favorite soups such as cream of mushroom and chicken noodle can not be canned. Noodles and anything that works to thicken the soup should be added later. Rice is another popular soup ingredient that can't be put in a pressure canner either.

Stock and broth are better and healthier when they are homemade rather than store bought. If you want to lower your sodium intake, homemaking and canning your own is a great way to do this. Broth that is made with meat will likely have higher amounts of fat. Before canning this type of broth, you are going to want to strain as much of this fat out as possible. If this is not done, the fat from the meat could float to the top of the jar and discolor the contents after the broth is canned. It could also turn the food rancid if it goes bad.

Mushrooms are another non-acidic food that can be pressure canned. While mushrooms are often seen as vegetables and are technically classified as such, I placed them in this category because they are not plants. However, they are the best food to have at a party. You know, because they are FUNGI. Get it? Anyway mushrooms are great to can due to their numerous health benefits. Just remember to be careful washing them as it may ruin the flavor and reduce its nutritional value. They also work really well in soups or stocks if you want to enhance the taste.

What Never to Can

Even though it is recommended to water bath can fruits, you can still use a pressure canner on them. The following foods can absolutely, under no circumstance, go through this method. Not only is it dangerous, but it will just result in the worst possible flavor outcomes. The first food, despite being non-acidic, is boiled eggs. Most people choose to preserve their eggs by pickling them, but unlike vegetables this doesn't make them ready for a water bath canner. In any method, the eggs are going to be overcooked and turned into a rubbery mess. Eggs can be used in a canner as an ingredient like, for instance, if you are canning lemon curd.

Milk, however, should never be used as an ingredient in something being canned. Milk is non-acidic which means it is the perfect place for the botulism bacteria. Even if it is processed in a pressure canner, the fat in milk preserves the *Botulinum* spores that will later turn into the toxin that has been known to kill. This is why dairy should never be canned in general. Anything else that comes from a cow that isn't meat, like butter, cheese, and cream should never see the inside of a canner. Dairy needs a great deal of heat to process and even if this temperature is reached, the food becomes inedible. Yogurt, sour cream, and even soy are off the table.

Grains don't make for very good canned goods either. There is little to no oil in grains, making them very dry. For other food, this is good because you don't want the oil to seep out after canning and ruin the product. It doesn't work the same for grains, though. Pressure canners will dry grains out further and destroy their nutritional value. It will also just ruin the flavor. Grains don't hold heat like other non-acidic foods, so their interior will not reach temperatures high enough to kill bacteria. This means you can not safely can any food that has rice, oats, bread, barley, crackers, dough, biscuits, or wheat.

Other foods that should be avoided are sweets with a lot of fat such as caramel and marshmallows. Like grain, they won't heat up properly, which allows for bacteria. Cornstarch and flour break down acid which is important for killing *Botulinum* spores. Pasta and noodles are made from flour and will just turn to mush. Nuts are too oily and this works against them as a protective layer to *Botulinum* spores. Lard has too much fat and it holds up well if it is frozen anyways. If you have canned any of these in the past and haven't gotten sick, you got lucky. Just because the potential is there doesn't always mean you'll get poisoned. Try to avoid these mistakes in the future because eventually you will lose at botulism roulette.

Chapter 6:

Pressure Canning Vegetables

Harvesting

Hardcore canners have their own garden where they can get the freshest of ingredients. This isn't mandatory for most recipes, but they will recommend it. There's no denying that fresher vegetables are better, if not just for the taste alone. They last longer, have more nutrients, and if you garden them yourself, you know what pesticides were used. Most grocery stores do offer an assortment of fresh vegetables, but keep in mind you don't always know if they are ethically sourced. You should always check them for bruises and brown spots before you make a purchase. Avoid the frozen isle, as there isn't much nutritional value there.

If you've decided that gardening is the best option for you, you will need to master the art of harvesting. Just because something looks ready, doesn't mean it always is. Every vegetable has its own peak for maturity. This will be the most opportune time to harvest. Picking before this could mean a less than favorable flavor. Picking after this peak could mean working with rotten food. When a vegetable has reached its largest stage that doesn't mean it is necessarily ripe. Other vegetables can be harvested before they are ripe. That's why you need to thoroughly research your veggies before you plant them.

If you are planning on pressure canning your vegetables, don't bother planting broccoli, cabbage, or cauliflower. They will lose their shape and become inedible mush. I suggest starting with carrots, peppers, and spinach. All of these have wonderful health benefits and are adaptable to most meals. Carrots are ready to be harvested when they are one inch in diameter. Spinach leaves are ready when they are at a length of four to six inches. Don't cut the crown if you wish to get several harvests out of the plant. Peppers come in different colors so you know what type you have for harvest. Bell peppers will be green and the usable hot peppers may be red or yellow when they ripen.

It is very important to keep your garden healthy. You can do this by avoiding bruising or damaging your produce while it's still on the vine. Stems and vines are fragile, so stepping on or injuring them, especially while they are wet, opens them up to potential diseases. This is why you should only harvest when it is dry out. If vegetables aren't being easily removed from their vine, use a clean knife instead of tugging at it as this could result in damage. Vegetables will still continue to grow way past their harvest date so make sure to keep up or they can quickly become overgrown.

Storing Vegetables

Most recipes are going to call for the freshest of produce and you should always try to can your vegetables as soon as possible. The farther you get from their harvesting date, the less nutrition and flavor you'll have. Sometimes, though, life doesn't go according to plan and you are going to need to store your vegetables. Fresher vegetables harvested from a home garden do better during storing than store bought vegetables. Not everybody has time or the space for a garden, though, so if you plan on storing store bought vegetables make sure they are damage free with little to no bruising.

There are several reasons as to why you might need to store vegetables before canning them. Just because something is in season, doesn't mean you have the time. If you have to wait a couple days after procuring your vegetables to can them, a refrigerator should be fine, but sometimes it might be weeks. Weather doesn't always permit either. Root vegetables like potatoes and carrots can be kept in the ground for longer, if need be. However, in wet and cold seasons they need to be quickly harvested. Another reason could be a recipe calls for mixed vegetables, but their harvest dates don't match up. You might need to store some spinach while you wait for your peppers to ripen.

There are a couple methods to storing vegetables safely. You can use your basement as long as it is cool and well ventilated. If you want to avoid the produce drying out, try placing them in moist sand. If you have room in your backyard, you can make an outdoor pit. Simply dig a hole and place an upright garbage can or wooden barrel in it. Make sure the top is four inches above the dirt. You'll want to dig a small moat around the perimeter to keep water out. Next, cover it in a foot of straw, grass clippings, or sawdust. The last step is placing a plastic cover over it. This should keep them cool and ripe for a couple of weeks.

Keep an eye on your stored produce. Just because these methods have worked for some people, doesn't mean something can't go wrong. Watch out for rot and remove any vegetables that show signs of going bad. A rotting vegetable can contaminate any vegetable nearby, so if you don't want to ruin the rest of your produce check them frequently. Clean the storage area thoroughly to avoid any unwanted contamination. If a vegetable looks shriveling, it's time to use it before it goes bad. Once a vegetable is taken out of storage it should be used right away.

Vegetables: Raw Pack vs. Hot Pack

Should vegetables be hot packed or raw packed? Oftentimes you won't have to make this decision yourself. Whatever recipe you choose, it is likely that it will say what is required of the specific meal you are planning. It is smarter to trust a well tested recipe than to make the decision on your own. However, in the case that the recipe doesn't specify what method to use, do not fret. There are ways to figure out what will work best for you. To make this decision you have to understand what each process is used for and what it does in relation to vegetables.

Hot packing is often used for water bath canning. It helps reduce the amount of oxygen and shrinks the food so you can get more contents into the jar. Hot pack canned goods keep their color and fresh flavor longer than their raw pack counterparts. This is because the food is boiled and then is left to simmer for a few minutes before it is placed in the jars for canning. The boiling is what removes the air and results in high quality food. It's important to make sure the jars aren't cooled before going into the canner or it runs the risk of coming out under-processed.

Raw packing is the process of canning the food without cooking it in any way first. Hot liquid is added over the contents before the jars are sealed. The food should be packed tight because it will start to shrink during the pressure canning process. There are four vegetables that are the exception to this rule and they are corn, potatoes, Lima beans, and peas. These veggies will expand and will need the extra room. Placing raw pack jars into a hot canning pot can break the glass so be wary of the temperature of the water inside your pressure canner.

Comparing the end result between the two methods, hot packing seems to be the more quality choice in relation to shelf life. Due to the fact that most vegetables shrink during the process, there ends up being empty space at the top of the jar where the air escapes to. This addition of air will lead to discoloration usually within three months. Hot packing however, is more work. This may seem worth it for better quality, but pre-boiling the vegetables is going to change the taste and texture anyways. Raw packing is usually recommended for specific food that is susceptible to losing its shape if it is hot packed.

Most vegetable canning recipes are going to recommend raw packing instead of hot packing. The USDA guidelines specifically state that raw packing is more suitable for vegetables. Does this mean you should only raw pack vegetables? No, there are a few deviations from this guideline. Potatoes should always be hot packed due to their starchy nature. If the starch isn't boiled out, it could leak from the potatoes and gelatinize the contents of the jar. Some canners also just prefer hot packing since the food becomes more pliable and is easier to fit in jars. This may be a better option for people with less jars to fill and don't want to waste anything.

Plain Vegetables

Plain vegetables must be pressure canned to avoid potential foodborne illness. If you want to make them safe for a water bath canner, you will need to pickle them by fermenting them in vinegar. This will not only change the acidic level, but also the taste. Before you place the vegetables in jars for pressure canning you should wash them, especially if they are garden fresh. Vegetables should be only rinsed off: If they are soaked in water, they will lose nutrition. When you are preparing the vegetables, be very gentle. Produce is fragile and you don't want to cause any bruising.

Carrots should be rinsed and peeled and rinsed again in preparation of the canning process. If you are canning baby carrots, they can be done whole but regular carrots should be sliced or diced. To hot pack carrots, boil them for five minutes before placing them in jars and pouring boiling water over them. To cold pack them just skip the part about pre-boiling them. Your recipe will tell you how long they should be processed and how pressure should be applied.

Corn can not be canned on the cob because it won't fit in the jar. You'll need to husk it, remove the excessive silk, and wash it before boiling it for three minutes. The corn can't be removed from the cob if it isn't boiled first. You can simply cut the kernels off but don't scrap them or you could ruin their form. You also have your choice of hot packing or cold packing them

If you want to can hot peppers, use gloves. You can wash your hands afterwards, but you really don't want to touch your face at any point during the preparation. They'll need to be washed as well. Since peppers come in all sizes, the little ones can be kept whole. You are going to want to slice up the bigger ones though. Remove their seeds and the core. Peppers should only be hot packed due to their thicker skin.

Potatoes should be washed, peeled, and then washed again. Potatoes can be left whole if they are very small but otherwise they should be cut up. Potatoes are very starchy which means, just like peppers, they should only be hot packed. You can get rid of this excess starch by boiling them for a couple of minutes depending on the size of your slices.

When you are jarring your vegetables, no matter what type they may be, only use the recipe recommended sizes. You can use smaller ones, but they might over cook. Just make sure to still follow the processing time listed. Larger jars are where the real safety issues come. Some vegetables will shrink during the canning process because of water loss, so keep that in mind when you pack them into the jars. In contrast to this, some will grow so make sure to know what you are working with and how they will react.

Mixed Vegetables

What's better than pressure canning one veggie at a time? Pressure canning mixed vegetables. This can and has been safely done for as long as the pressure canner has been around. The most common combinations are carrots, peas, green beans, corn, tomatoes, and summer squash, but as long as you can can it, feel free to be creative. While tomatoes are considered a fruit, they pair better with veggies. If you plan on doing so you'll have to use a pressure canner. The acidic nature of tomatoes is not going to make corn any more safe in a water bath canner.

Make sure to pick the right recipe when it comes to mixing vegetables. The more complicated a process is, the more important it is to find a well trusted source to get your recipe from. If you are using a recipe and plan on making any sort of substitution, be careful that it won't drastically change the outcomes. For instance, if you're mixing carrots and potatoes, but the recipe calls for carrots and green beans to be cold packed, then you're gonna need to change that too.

Pressure canning mixed vegetables is going to take a longer preparation time. Make sure you know what to do for each vegetable. Pay attention to your recipe as it will help you navigate and prevent possible confusion from this. Some of the same rules may apply, like rinsing instead of soaking, and what size pieces to cut them into. Depending on your choice of vegetable, you might have the decision on whether to cold or hot pack them. This might be done together or separately. If you are combining potatoes or peppers with non-starching food, you'll still need to hot pack it.

The PSI and processing times are going to change, too. Different vegetables are going to require longer times that can overcook other vegetables. The tested recipe is going to try its best to avoid this, but it still can be a possible side effect of canning mixed vegetables. Make sure your recipe is specific to your type of canner and altitude as well. You don't want to put all this work in for nothing.

Chapter 7:

Pressure Canning Stock

What Is Stock?

Surprisingly, there's been much debate on the difference between stock, soup, and broth. The average Joe probably thinks they are all the same. Are they right? The answer is actually still up in the air. Most chefs tend to agree that soup could be either broth or stock as long as they are served as a dish with added ingredients such as vegetables, meats, and grains. Another term that gets thrown around with this topic of conversation is bouillon. Is this another predecessor to soup like the other terms? Yes, it is because bouillon is just another word for broth.

So, what's the difference between stock and broth? In the eyes of a classically trained chef, stock is made from bones and vegetables like onions, carrots, or celery. It can be made from any animal, but most come from the bones of chicken or cows. It has seasoning and its flavor comes from roasting the bones. Stock's most defining feature is its very thick texture. In cooler temperatures, this thickness becomes gelatinous. This is because of the collagen in the connective tissue of the bones. Stock isn't usually eaten as is and works as a base to start off soups and sauces.

Broth is the byproduct of actual meat. It is liquid that meat has been cooked in and uses the same vegetables as stock. It also doesn't matter what meat is being used in the liquid. Chicken is the most common type of broth, but beef is a close second. As for what part, once again, the answer is any. Some people make it with a whole chicken carcass. Whereas stock has a viscous texture, broth is more watery. It is also made with seasoning and can be served just as it is. Broth can be a base and be actual soup.

The main difference between the two is that broths are made with meat, and stocks are made with bones. Here is where it gets confusing, though. The term bone broth is just another name for stock and isn't considered a broth by professional chefs. If broth or stock is prepared vegetarian style, they are the same thing because veggies don't have bones or meat. When it comes to canning these foods, none of this information makes a difference. Stock, broth, or soup are considered non-acidic and should always be canned using a pressure canner.

The Basics of Stock Safety

You don't have to butcher your own chickens to make homemade broth or stock, but you can. The healthiest and best flavored broths come from free range chickens. Most chickens are slaughtered at 47-days old. Make sure you fully pluck and clean the chicken before using it's carcass. Chickens tend to be clean animals, but that doesn't mean they don't get sick. If it's going to be butchered, the animal needs to be in perfect health. It's also important to prepare the meat in a timely manner. Don't wait for the chicken to rot before you start cleaning it up.

Sometimes killing a chicken just isn't for you or maybe you just don't have the space to raise them. It takes a lot of work that may seem unnecessary when you can get fresh meat from your local butcher. This is the easier alternative if you prefer beef stock anyways. Frozen meat can be used to make broth and stock but it's not going to taste as good so make sure to use fresher meat. You should also know what farm your meat is coming from and how they raise their livestock. As stated above, free range chickens are often the preference.

Since stocks and broth can be made from just about any type of meat, going to the butcher or raising your own chickens are not the only options. Stock can be made from any leftover meat you have around the house. You can use the remains of a half eaten rotisserie chicken, steak bones, shells from any type of seafood, or even the last piece of fried chicken from a combo meal. Will these make top quality broths? Probably not, but you can try it. As long as the meat hasn't been sitting out and has started to spoil, you can use whatever meat product you want.

Stocks and broths have a lot of fat in them. To reduce this you can chill the broth for 12 or more hours. In this time, the fat will float to the top and all you have to do is skim what you don't want off. You can always keep the fat and use it for cooking or additional flavors. Leaving the fat in might raise your cholesterol, but won't cause any problems as long as you eat the broth within the first six months after it is canned. If you're worried that the fat might grease up the lid and ruin the seal, rub vinegar around the rim.

The Benefits of Canning Stock

Despite what gourmet chefs say, you can pretty much do whatever you want when it comes to making stock. Throw some meat, veggies, and seasoning into some water and let it simmer. If you are a vegetarian, you don't even have to use meat. It is completely up to you on what type of stock you want. This means you can control the flavor, the nutrition, and the amount made. It is pretty easy to make too much stock and that is where the blessing that is canning comes in. Stock is made from non-acidic foods and has to be canned in a pressure canner.

Since broth and stocks are pretty easy to make and work well as a staple to most diets, many people can them by the gallon. This is no problem as long as you have the room and your canner has the capacity to do so. It might take a lot of time, but at least you'll have a year's supply. Then you'll only ever have to make it once a year, so in a way it saves you time and money spent on ingredients. Store bought bone broth can get a little expensive, so having it readily available without the worry of spoilage is also another financial benefit.

Perhaps, most famously, bone broth has a lot of health benefits. The gelatin protein found in bone broths works to help regulate the digestive system. Bone broth may help with certain gut issues, too, such as IBS, but not much research has been done on the subject. The intestines can directly affect the immune system, and so consuming bone broth can possibly protect you against certain food borne illnesses. Drinking bone broth will not shield you from botulism though, so don't try to can it in a water bath canner. In one research trial with mice, bone broth helped to increase microbial diversity.

Another health benefit of stock is its collagen properties. Collagen is often used as a supplement in skin care routines to look younger and more refreshed. Consuming a large amount of bone broth has shown to increase levels of the amino acids that create collagen. This has led to claims that stock can have anti-aging effects. Another benefit of collagen is its improvement of pain and stiffness of joints in patients with osteoarthritis. The gelatin found in collagen has even been found to prevent exercise injuries.

Chicken Broth vs. Beef Broth

Bone broth has recently gained popularity in the health-conscious community. It has even replaced coffee as a morning supplement in some households. With all the new research coming forward about it's miraculous properties, it makes one wonder which broth is better, chicken or beef? As far as flavor is concerned, that is up to you. When it comes to meat, chicken and beef have always been at odds. They are both commonly found in American meals and have proven themselves versatile. No matter which broth you prefer, you will still reap the health benefits.

Starting with chicken, it is the easier option to make due to it being the number one consumed meat in the U.S. and Canada. Chicken bones are more readily available than cow bones. They are less dense, so it doesn't take as long to cook chicken broth up. Chicken bones are what are linked to the joint relief properties recorded in patients with osteoarthritis. It also produces amino acids that make collagen and repairs skin damage. Despite the limited research into its reproduction of collagen available, chicken broth has several celebrity endorsements. Chicken broth has more protein, but it also has more cholesterol.

Beef has a longer cooking time due to the density of cow bones. Since they aren't as available as chicken bones, they are more expensive. The health benefit most related to beef broth is regulating intestines and promoting gut health. Beef has more amino acids that produce glycine. Glycine is good for your gut because it fights inflammation. Glycine also helps you sleep and relax, which is shown to boost your mood by increasing serotonin. Beef's flavor is often considered to be more bold than chicken flavor. Some people find this more satisfying.

In the end, it might just come down to what you're in the mood for. Sometimes chicken sounds better than beef and other times it's the opposite. As far as benefits go, chicken has beef beat. It has more protein, hydrating electrolytes and muscle building amino acids. However, if you have high cholesterol, you are going to want to go with beef. You should also go with beef if you want to fight seasonal depression with a warm mug of bone broth. Older people might prefer to look younger with chicken broth's age-defying magic. I find that with all these potential benefits, the best solution is to drink both.

Tips for Canning Broth

Here is a tip that might be controversial to some world renowned chefs. The difference between broth and stock doesn't matter. It shouldn't limit how you choose to prepare this dish. Add meat to your bone broth, add bones to your meat broth. Don't have any meat products at all and just use vegetables. They are both nutritious and there's no reason why you can't have seasoning and a thick texture. It's safe and makes the stock taste better. It feels almost pretentious to pretend that they are different. Do whatever works for your pallet.

While fat isn't the worst thing to eat, it is one of the worst things to can. Your broth will go bad within six months, but it could also go bad right away. The grease in fat can ruin a seal and then the stock that was supposed to last a year won't even last a week. A little bit of fat is going to be inevitable, but it shouldn't affect the final product. If you want to avoid your broth going rancid, removing the fat with the previously mentioned method is your best choice.

With any food that is going to be canned and stored for almost a year, fresher ingredients are better. You can buy bone broth from the store with the intention to can it, but homemade stock will usually taste better and have a longer shelf life. It also has more health benefits. If you do decide this is the best option for you, you are going to need to find a recipe for canning bone broth that most closely resembles the ingredients you used. Seafood stock is going to have a different processing time than vegetable stock.

It's very easy to can a lot of stock but you should only do this if you need a lot of stock. Canning by the gallons is going to take up a large amount of space.

Space that can be used for carrot, potatoes and spinach. Your caning pantry should be diverse. One main point to canning is to be able to eat foods that are out of season and to add an assortment of nutritious foods that wouldn't be available otherwise. Stock is healthy but only eating stock will stunt your diet.

Chapter 8: Bonus Chapter -
Pressure Canning Meat

The Basics of Meat Safety

Fresh meat makes the best meat. If you are not providing your own meat, make sure to only purchase from the meat counter at the grocery store or your local butcher shop. Purchasing from the frozen aisle will result in less flavor. At the store, it is best if you purchase the freshest food last. Make sure the product is cold because warm temperatures can cause rapid deterioration of the product. Pay attention to the sell-by-dates listed on the packaging. Meat that is within two days of it's sell-by-date should be canned right away.

Canning should be done as quickly as possible but this isn't always an attainable goal. If you plan on refrigerating the meat, do this as soon as you return home. If meat is exposed to room temperature for more than 30 minutes, it can start to go bad. Only purchase from grocery stores nearby or keep the meat in an ice cooler during transportation. If you are freezing meat, make sure to protect it from freezer burn with a thicker layer of packaging. Keep in mind frozen meat loses its flavor and won't taste as good when canned.

When it is time for preparation, you can not defrost meat at room temperature or bacteria can grow. Place them in the refrigerator so it will stay cold as it defrosts. You can also defrost the meat by putting it in cold water. Make sure it is in an airtight bag though because you don't want to contaminate the meat with unwanted moisture. If you are short on time, a microwave can also work. However, the meat should be cooked directly after this to prevent any bacteria that can thrive off the warm parts of the meat.

If you are planning to can the meat with vegetables, do not share utensils between them. Clean anything that has touched the meat before it works with the vegetables. They should not be prepared within five feet of each other to avoid cross contamination. You will also need to wash your hands after touching the meat. Meat can only ever be safely canned in a pressure canner because it is non-acidic. A water bath canner will not be hot enough to kill the *Botulinum* spores.

Meat: Raw Pack vs. Hot Pack

Choosing whether to raw pack or hot pack meat is very similar to choosing a method for vegetables. For safety reasons, meat can only ever be canned in a pressure canner. A water bath canner does not get hot enough to kill off the potential bacteria of botulism and other dangerous contaminations. The raw pack method works best with most food used in a pressure canner and so it's likely that most recipes will suggest this. Just because this is what is recommended by the USDA doesn't mean this is the only option. Meat can be safely hot packed and choosing to do so will not lead to any serious repercussions.

The choice is up to you and that's why knowing the pros and cons of each method is paramount to your food enjoyment. Once again, hot packing anything will take more preparation. Instead of boiling the food like you do with vegetables or fruit, meat is precooked in some way. This is mostly just basic browning of the meat and since the pressure canner reaches a high level of heat, you don't need to cook it all the way through. After the meat is cooked and placed in the jars, boiled broth, drippings, water, or tomato juice are added on top.

Raw packing meat, just like raw packing vegetables, is a much simpler process. Cut up the meat however you want to and if desired add salt. Canned meat is usually cut into cubes, strips or regular chunks. Raw packing meat doesn't require liquid because liquid is naturally stored within raw meat and is cooked out during the hot pack process. Not all meat has enough liquid to cover all the contents in the jar and that is when discoloration happens. Since there is no liquid added with the raw packing method, leave two to three centimeters of space in between the top of the jar and the meat. This room is for the meat's liquid secretion and prevents the jars from becoming too full.

Whichever method you choose, the processing time is the same. This means that if you're short on time, a raw pack method might be the better option for you. However, if you have a finite amount of jars, once again hot packing will be better since the meat shrinks when it's cooked. Raw packed meat also ends up looking less full in comparison because of this. Hot packing also allows for the separation between meat and fat. Raw packs often have more fat at the top of their jars that can make the food go rancid.

One worry you might have about raw packing is whether the meat will be fully cooked. The answer is yes, you can eat the meat directly from the jar after processing. Unlike vegetables, raw packing is said to have a better taste and texture compared to hot packing. There is only one meat where the choice isn't yours and that is ground beef. Ground beef must be hot packed because its consistency is too clumpy and won't cook all the way. Make sure to shape the ground beef and cook it just enough that you won't have to worry about it congealing into a dense mass.

Meat Products

Meat products refers to any meat that does not fall under the category of seafood or poultry such as beef, venison, lamb or pork. Meat has high levels of fat and that needs to be removed before the canning process begins. If this fat isn't removed, the jar might not seal. If it hasn't been done already, bones will need to be removed. Wild meat will have a stronger flavor which means it should be soaked in brine for one hour. The ideal ratio of this brine will be one tablespoon of salt per quart of water

Meat can be cut into cubes, strips or chunks depending on whatever you prefer. These pieces should be no more than one inches wide to ensure even cooking throughout the meat. If you are canning wild game make sure you will have enough jars and lids. It is also important to have an assortment of canned goods so it is necessary to have room in your canning pantry for more than just this meat. Only can as many jars at a time as is recommended in your owner's manual.

Cold packed jars full of meat often lose water so to ensure it cooks and doesn't become discolored, hot packing is usually the best way to prepare meat products. The choice is up to you, though. If you want to hot pack, start by pre-cooking the meat. You can roast it, stew it or brown it until it is rare. Add salt and pack it into hot jars. You should leave a one inch headspace at the top. Before you close the jar, add in your choice of boiling liquid. The raw process is the same procedure, except you skip the precooking stage.

Whether you are using a weighted gauge or a pressure gauge canner, it will usually take 90 minutes to process if you have quart jars. Pints only take 75 minutes. The

PSI will change depending on your altitude but anywhere under 1,000 feet is doing 11 PSI for a dial gauge and 10 for a weighted. Anywhere that is above 1,000 feet in a weighted gauge will raise to 15 PSI. Jar size does not affect PSI.

Poultry and Rabbit

Poultry is defined as the meat that is harvested from domestic fowls. This includes goose, chicken, duck, turkey and game bird. Rabbit meat can and should be canned the same way as poultry. For the best taste, you will want to procure the meat from a free range farm. Poultry should be chilled 6 to 12 hours before it is canned. Rabbit needs to be soaked in salt water for an hour before it is canned. The ratio of this salt water bath should be one tablespoon of salt per quart of water. You should also remove any excess fat to ensure the sealing process works correctly.

Because their bones are small, poultry and rabbit meat can be canned with or without bones. This will change the processing time for the two products. Cut the poultry or rabbit meat into small pieces that fit into whatever jar size you will be using. Poultry and rabbit have similar procedures to meat products when it comes to hot packing or cold packing. To avoid any liquid loss, hot packing is recommended but not mandatory.

To hot pack poultry or rabbit meat, you can boil or bake until they are about two-thirds done. Fill the jars, leaving a 1-1/4 inch headspace. If you want to enhance the flavor, you can add a teaspoon of salt. Add less if you are using pint jars. Lastly add hot broth and make sure to keep the 1-1/4 inch headspace. Cold pack is exactly the same without the precooking or the addition of broth.

If you have a dial-gauge pressure canner process the jars at 11 PSI at altitudes below 2,000 feet or at 12 PSI for altitudes of 2,001 to 4,000 feet. If you have a weighted gauge pressure canner, you should process jars at 10 PSI for altitudes below 1,000 ft. For altitudes above 1,000 feet, 15 PSI is ideal. Both raw pack and hot pack will take 75 minutes for pints and 90 minutes for quarts if you took out the bones. Processing times for poultry and rabbits that still have bones are 65 minutes for pints and 75 minutes for quarts.

Seafood

Unlike poultry or meat, seafood doesn't have one method to properly cook everything. You will have to pay special attention to what your recipe says to do because everything is specialized. The processing time for seafood is also much longer than their counterparts. Where pints take about 75 minutes for meat, they take 110 minutes for some seafood. This is because seafood is at a higher risk for botulism than meat or poultry especially if it is shell bearing. Whether a fish is smoked or not will change the processing time.

Some sources approve of using the quart jar but most recipes favor the pint jar for canning seafood. Smoked fish should always be canned in pint jars only. A popular jar for seafood is the half pint jar, nicknamed the salmon jar. If you decide to can in a quart jar, venting times will need to be extended to 30 minutes. Smaller pressure canners such as the All-American 10.5 quart and 15.5 quart models are not permitted to safely can smoked fish. Smoked fish should not be thoroughly cooked before canning or you run the risk of drying it out.

If you are worried about discoloration, you can add lemon juice to the fish before canning them. This won't help preservation but it will keep the fish from turning dark. When preparing the fish, cut off the head, tail and fin. The bones will become soft and edible. You have the choice to remove or keep the skin on. If you want the jar to look more aesthetic, you can have the skin facing out but if you want an easier clean turn it in.

Fish can be frozen before they are canned like other meat but when it comes to defrosting them, it can only be done in a fridge. It is important to rinse the thawed fish off when it is done to get rid of any icicles. Another thing you should do is avoid reprocessing seafood. If a jar doesn't seal the first time around, the second time will just overcook it. At this point, there is no other option than to dispose of the jar's contents.

Chapter 9:

Caring for Your Pressure Canner

Basic Maintenance

Maintenance for your pressure canner can come in all forms. Whether it is cleaning, replacing parts, or even just double checking that everything is working, maintenance is a vital part of the canning process. Canning is often seasonal work done when the product is ready to harvest. This means that for a good amount of the year, the pressure canner is not being used. This time is just as important as the productive period when it comes to maintenance. Pressure canners can be expensive and that's why purchasing one should be an investment. If you don't keep it from getting ruined, then it won't last as long as it can.

A simple maintenance tip is cleaning before and after every use. This may be annoying to do every time, but it is better to be safe than sorry. Dirty pots are the perfect breeding ground for bacteria that you don't want anywhere near your food. It's not just the pot that you should clean, either. The lid and gasket will need a thorough rinse. Rubber is not as durable as metal and keeping it clean is one way to make it last as long as possible. Make sure to remove the canning rack from the pot and clean it separately so you don't miss any spots.

Every so often, you will need to spend money on replacements. The most common of these replacements is the biennial gasket replacement. Some gaskets can last five years but waiting two years in between changes is more often recommended. As previously stated, rubber is not a strong material and once it starts to crack, the chances of your pressure canner blowing a gasket rises. Since this is the most common replacement, gaskets are very cheap and easy to find. If you have an All-American brand pressure canner, you won't have to ever worry about getting new gaskets since they have a metal to metal seal feature.

Another thing that you should do to keep up with maintenance is annual dial gauge checks. If you over-process your jars due to an inaccurate dial gauge the taste is more than likely going to be sub-par. If you under-process your jars you could die. This may sound dramatic, but unfortunately it's true. While botulism is very rare, it is still a serious condition that should be avoided at all costs. Your local extension service can help with your annual check. If you have a weighted gauge then you won't have to worry about this potential problem.

Maintenance can be boring and repetitive, but canners that are well cared for can last up to several decades. There are many moving parts, which means there is a lot of work to be done to keep these machines safe. Make sure to thoroughly read your owner's manual to find any other things you should be regularly doing to care for your pressure canner. Maintenance also depends on your model so if you are not someone with a lot of time to do this, you can always buy a model that seals without a gasket and uses the weighted gauge feature. No matter what model you have, you should still always clean it frequently.

Part Replacement

It is important to know when to call it quits on your pressure canner parts. The signs are different depending on what needs to be replaced. If you are confused on whether or not something needs to be changed, your trusty owner's manual should give you an idea. If your model has any rubber, they are going to need to be replaced more often than any of the metal parts. The main indicator for rubber is a brittle texture, while metal should be replaced if it has completely rusted over. To avoid accidents, don't use pieces that exhibit these signs.

Once you know what you're replacing, you can usually find a new one online by looking up your brand and model. Presto pressure canners will often have a model number stamped on the side or on the bottom of the pot. This number will tell you exactly what type of part you will need to match your pressure canner. If you don't have a Presto, the owner's manual will have or say where you can find the model number. You don't want to just guess your model number because the wrong part could cause the canning process to go south.

Since gaskets are the most often replaced part, you should know how to do it. The first step is taking off the old gasket and cleaning the groove. This is an easy spot for residue to hide, so make sure to scrub at any leftover soap or potential rust. Before the new gasket is installed it needs to be washed with warm, soapy water. Rinse it and then let it soak for 10 minutes to increase it's pliability. It needs to be completely dried so it won't rust the groove. When installing the new gasket, work it in with one section of the groove at a time.

You should also replace the pressure plug every time you change the gasket since they are both made out of rubber. Much of the process of changing this out is the same as the gasket. You should remove the old piece and clean the air vent out thoroughly. Clean the new plug in the same way with soapy water and dry it to prevent rust. Different canners will require different ways to insert the new plug into the vent. Carefully read the instructions before you attempt to do so as to avoid accidentally ruining the new plug.

With all these required replacements, you might be wondering how much they cost. The price of a pressure canner can be upwards of 200 dollars and it might seem like a continuous drain on your wallet to keep it working. The only reason why the actual canners are that expensive is because they last a long time. Most replacement parts are very cheap and easy to find online. Whether it is a gasket, a pressure plug or a dial gauge, you can find it for under 20 dollars on Amazon or from your brand's direct website.

Cleaning

All the parts of the pressure canner need to be cleaned. We've gone over cleaning the vent pipe and safety valve, but what about the actual lid? Unless you are using your pressure canner as a cooker, there shouldn't be any food sticking to the inside of the lid, but you still check to make sure it is perfectly clean. Your type of gauge will tell you if soaking the lid is a good idea or not. A dial-gauge can rust or corrode if it is ever immersed in water. Also avoid holding the dial-gauge upside down when your lid is being washed or it could end up collecting moisture and ruining the dial's capability to tell pressure.

Certain chemicals such as lye, scouring powder, or baking soda can stain aluminum pots and should never be used to clean your pressure canner. When your canner is in the cooling process let it come down to low temperature naturally. Adding cold water can warp the shape of your canner and make the lid no longer close correctly. This will make the pressure canner unsafe to use. Never leave any liquid or food in the pot for extended periods of time. If your pot is made from aluminum it will likely absorb any strange odors that will be difficult to get rid of.

Mineral deposits are an unfortunate occurrence, but they're not the end of the world. A dark line around the perimeter of the canner can be removed with a mixture of water and cream of tartar. This should be measured as one tablespoon of tartar for every quart of water. Fill the pot with this mixture so that it is covering the mineral deposit. Heat this on the stove until it boils the stain away. Add more cream of tartar if it doesn't work. Once it looks like it has cleared up, empty the canner and wash it with hot, soap water. The last step is to rinse and dry thoroughly

This process can be tedious after a while but there are ways to prevent mineral deposits from forming in the first place. Adding two tablespoons of white vinegar to the canner's water before you start pressurizing should do the trick. Sometimes the cream of tartar method for cleaning the pressure canner doesn't work and you have to do it several times to see results, so it's better to prevent this than fix it later. Preventative care initiatives like this one are an important way to make your pressure canner last longer and work more efficiently.

Caring for Utensils

Jars and their lids are probably the most essential utensil to the canning process. You can't can if you don't have a can to can the canned goods in. We've already gone over basic jar care in Chapter 3, but a reminder to clean and routinely check for cracks doesn't hurt. Also, remember to throw away the tops after one use, but you can reuse the jar and screw band. Jars aren't the only canning utensil that requires care and attention: Don't forget to consider the needs of other equipment, so that you won't have to keep spending money to replace items that can easily last you years.

Tongs are just as susceptible to rust as any other metal part of the canner. Always dry them off completely before putting them in storage. If they do start to rust, you can always use water and baking soda to break down these deposits. Scrub with a wire brush afterwards. If your tongs touch any food and it isn't properly washed off, they could grow mold. Soapy water and some light scrubbing after use will help to prevent this. Other metal equipment, such as a steel funnel should be subjected to this same care routine.

Some of your equipment might have rubber handles or other parts made from this material. As we have gone over multiple times, rubber is not as strong as metal. It needs a more gentle cleaning ritual. Don't use any brushes that are made from metal or they will rip it up. A regular, soft, yellow sponge will do just fine. Don't put the rubber near any high temperature heat sources or it could melt. Worn down rubber is an easy spot for bacteria to grow so make sure to either replace that part or if need be, the whole thing.

Canning is very messy at times and so you're going to need kitchen washcloths to wipe down jars and countertops where the food is prepared. You could use paper towels, but they're not very good for the environment. It is also financially beneficial to work with reusable supplies. Fabric can easily develop mold or spread bacteria so don't use dirty cloths. This goes for oven mitts as well. There's a lot of hot surfaces that you might have to touch so you'll definitely need one of these. Don't forget to wash it after you use it.

Storing

When the harvest season comes to an end, it's time to put your canning equipment away until next year. Pressure canners are meant to last decades, but that doesn't mean you can just put it anywhere and it will be in perfect condition a year later. They require care and a good amount of attention. You won't want to start off the next canning season with a rusty pressure canner and broken utensils. Even if you have the perfect location to keep the canner, there's still a whole procedure to follow before you can store it. Skipping any step could shorten your equipment's lifespan.

Clean the entire pot for good measure. Any leftover residue can make the pot rust and develop mold if you give it enough time. You'll also want to dislodge anything that might be trapped in the vent pipe with a pipe cleaner. The overpressure plug should be removed and the area should be scrubbed for rust. Remember to put the plug back in though, as you don't want to lose such a small piece. Don't forget about the utensils. The canning rack, jars, jar lifter and other special canning equipment need to be washed and dried before it is ready to be stored.

The appliance is still not ready to be stored until you've checked everything's condition. Any rubber piece needs to be looked over for breakage or any brittle parts. If you need to replace a gasket, wait until next year so that it isn't already a year old by the time you get to use it. The dial gauge doesn't need to be checked at the local extension service until right before next harvest season. You should still look for cracks in the glass or other damage. The pot and lid should be inspected for any signs of rust because that needs to be taken care of as soon as possible.

After everything is checked over and cleaned, it is finally time to store your canner and canning supplies. Crumple up some clean paper towels and put them in the bottom of the pot with the rack. This will work to absorb moisture and unwanted odors. The lid can be placed on top of the canner upside down. Don't seal it on or that might lead to mold growth. Jars should be stored without their lids and placing them upside down will limit dust deposits. Pressure canners need to be stored in clean and dry areas. Follow all these steps and you'll be ready for the next canning season.

Chapter 10:

What's the Worst That Could Happen?

Botulism

So, what is the worst that could happen if you don't use a pressure canner safely? Death. The most dangerous thing to worry about isn't an explosion, it is a foodborne illness. If your jars are not properly sealed, you run the risk of creating the perfect environment for the *Clostridium botulinum* bacteria. This bacteria produces a serious toxin that causes the illness of botulism. The toxin is produced in food, wounds, and baby intestines. Luckily this is a rare condition, but it should still be taken seriously. If, for whatever reason, you may believe you have contracted botulism, seek medical attention immediately.

The bacteria that causes botulism isn't actually that dangerous. It's naturally found in many different places and isn't found to cause any illness. It's the spores created by the bacteria that become dangerous. The spores are produced to protect the bacteria in harsh conditions such as low oxygen or low acid levels. Since pressure canners are used for non-acidic food products, there's always the possibility for these spores to spawn. When the spores themselves are consumed, it is still unlikely to get sick with botulism. It's only when the spores grow and produce the toxin that problems arise. As long as the food is properly canned, the spores won't grow or produce the toxin.

Botulism has clear signs and symptoms to look out for. If you fear you might have consumed contaminated food, pay attention to your eyes. If your vision is blurry or you feel like you are seeing double, these are red flags. More optical issues include difficulty moving your eyes or drooping eyelids. Another area you should pay attention to is your stomach. If you are nauseous, vomiting, or having other stomach related issues botulism is a possibility. Other symptoms include muscle weakness and problems with breathing, swallowing, and speech. It is possible to not show signs of all of these symptoms and still have botulism.

If you do seek medical attention, the doctor will likely perform a series of tests before diagnosis. These include a brain scan, a spinal fluid examination, and nerve and muscle function tests. However, the only way to know for certain is a specific laboratory test. Depending at what stage you are at, treatment will vary. You will firstly be administered an antitoxin drug to stop any further damage from the toxin. This is not a cure all though, and won't reverse the effects you've already suffered. Botulism attacks the nervous system and can cause paralysis. Most patients slowly recover, but this can take weeks or even months. In the case of a patient with breathing issues, a ventilator may be administered until they can breathe on their own.

Less than 5 of every 100 people with botulism die. This is far better than in the past when the survival rate was only 50%. The most common complication of botulism is respiratory failure. Many problems can arise from long term paralysis as well such as infection. Years after their diagnosis, some patients still report shortness of breath and fatigue. Pressure canners were created precisely to avoid this illness. As long as you pay attention to the USDA's safety protocols in relation to the pressure canner, you will never have to deal with this food poisoning.

Avoiding Contamination

The most important toxin to look out for is botulism, but fortunately it and other contaminants can be easily avoided. There is no way to taste, see, or smell the botulism toxin, but one little bite can kill you so it's important to know other ways to avoid this deadly mistake. Always remember to sterilize everything: One contaminated tool and it's all over. Sterilizing couldn't be more simple, just place your jars, tongs, and lids in boiling water heated up on the stove. This will kill any dangerous bacteria and make your work space safe for canning. Jars should be immersed in boiling water for at least ten minutes.

The USDA provides a complete guide to home canning that should be scrupulously followed. During the canning process, cutting corners is highly dangerous. No amount of money, resources, or time is worth your life. Canning beginners shouldn't even buy a pressure canner before reading these techniques. Even if you have a lot of experience with canning but are just getting back into it after taking time away, don't trust your memory. Review the guidelines, they are there to keep you safe. Other reading material about canning safety can be provided by the National Center for Home Food Preservation or your state and county extension services.

A sure-fire way to make sure your food isn't contaminated is to use the right equipment. Low acid foods need to be pressure canned. A pressure cooker or just using the water bath method will not have good results. Even if the cooker has a feature for canning, the size difference between the two appliances makes it unsafe. Pressure canners can be expensive, but so are hospital bills. It's also important to make sure your equipment is in working condition. Before each use, always check the gauge's accuracy and that the gasket isn't starting to crumble. If you are unsure how to check your gauge, county extension services can do it for you.

Just because you can't physically see botulism doesn't mean you can't see the signs of contamination. If you pick up a jar off your shelf and it looks swollen or the lid is bulging, do not eat its contents. Whether you canned it months ago or yesterday, the food has gone bad and is no longer safely edible. Avoid eating discolored, or foaming substances. Always trust your nose when it comes to canned goods. If a jar's contents smell rancid or moldy, throw it out. In fact, if you have any reason to doubt the food's safety then throw it out.

Jars are the most important indicator for any possible contamination. Through every part of the canning process make sure your jars are in good condition. One little scratch isn't going to make a difference but a chip on the rim could completely affect the sealing process and allow bacteria to grow. Also keep in mind that just because jars are reusable doesn't mean their lids are. Most lids are not manufactured with the ability to reseal jars after they've already been used. Once again, if the jar isn't sealed bacteria can grow and produce the botulism toxin.

Understanding Food Acid Levels

Knowing the difference between a water bath canner and a pressure canner is the first step to not contracting botulism. A water bath canner is for acidic food and a pressure canner is for low or non-acidic food. This basic fact is helpful, but how can you tell what foods are acidic and what aren't? Well it's pH levels, of course. To anyone who doesn't study agriculture or food safety, this means nothing. What are pH levels? Taste isn't always an indicator for whether foods are acidic. You have to look at it on an atomic level. Acid releases free hydrogen ions and pH levels are just a scale to measure these free hydrogen ions in food.

This scale is pretty much useless if you don't know how to read it. It ranges from zero to 14, zero being the most acidic and 14 being non-acidic. For better understanding, battery acid is a zero while liquid drain cleaner is a 14. The pH level seven is considered to be neutral. This is the acidic level of pure water. If a level is above seven, it is called alkaline. Most food that can be processed in a pressure canner isn't actually alkaline and sits at a range a little lower than seven. Alkaline will sometimes also be called basic.

Food with a pH level above 4.6 needs to be pressure canned or it can become the breeding ground for *Botulinum* spores. This rule was made specifically because of this bacteria. Fruits can usually kill these spores, but meat and vegetables can't. It's usually a safe bet to only pressure can foods with high pH and only water bath food with low pH. With any rule comes the exception, so make sure to research your product before you start to can it. This rule doesn't always take into account food viscosity, taste, or heat transfer properties though.

Not all foods that are considered to be acidic should be canned in a water bath canner alone. Tomato, the most indecisive of produce, requires an addition of lemon juice. This is because their pH levels are near 4.6. Other borderline foods such as the papaya and figs have a similar pH level and also need a supplement to increase their acidic levels. Cantaloupe and watermelon have pH levels that match some kinds of meat. Pressure canning these isn't recommended though, because it will ruin the flavor. They can only be water bath canned once they've been pickled.

Will My Pressure Canner Explode?

No. It can, but it won't because you know how to avoid it. You have purchased a pressure canner that is not older than your grandparents, and therefore should have a release valve. You also frequently clean your equipment, so you never have to worry about dirt or other unwanted particles blocking the safety valve. If you own a dial-gauge, you get it checked every year so you won't accidentally apply too much pressure in your pot. You've also read through your owner's manual and keep it around in case something goes wrong. Most importantly you've read this book. The only way your pressure canner is going to explode is if you let it.

There are three common defects, all of which you can avoid. The first problem that can cause an explosion is an unsealed lid. If a lid isn't sealing, don't turn it on. You don't want the steam to escape in an uncontrolled way or for the lid to go flying. There are numerous reasons as to why a lid won't shut. The canner can be too full or something may be lodged in the gasket.

Something could have warped the pot as well. In this case, you'll have to get a new pressure canner.

The next problem is a faulty gasket. Gaskets seal the canner's lid. If you gasket breaks in the middle of a load the lid can pop off and you can get burned. This is unlikely to happen if you replace your gasket every year. If this happens and you have a new gasket, you may have gotten the wrong size. Make sure to look up your make and model in your pressure canner owner's manual. The last defect and most unlikely is insufficient venting. This only happens when something clogs both the overpressure plug and the vent pipe.

It's unlikely that your canner will come with a manufacturing error that causes any of these problems, but it is possible. Make sure to check all your parts are working after you purchase the canner even if it's not second hand. You might get a good settlement, but you'll also get burned so it is always better to be safe than sorry. An explosion is probably not going to cause any more damage than within a 10 foot radius, so if you notice steam isn't coming out properly, turn the appliance off and run away.

How to Spot Danger

You can store most home canned goods for up to one year. Anything older than this should be swapped out for something new. This is why labeling your products with the date they were canned is very important. Always have a well-organized canned goods storage so you know when something is about to go over one year. Does this mean you can't eat canned food that is older than a year? No, you can. Once it is properly canned, the food is technically edible forever as long as the seal isn't broken. Is it going to taste good forever? No. Quality and nutrition drop after one year.

If you want your canned goods to retain their quality for as long as possible, have a regulated temperature between 50 and 70 degrees Fahrenheit where you store them. Anything higher than 95 degrees will shorten the shelf life. The food won't become toxic but it will spoil. If you think your food has spoiled, don't taste test it. Jars that are stored without screw bands will have a clear indication of something wrong. As a rule of thumb, If the seal is broken, the food has gone bad. Bacteria and yeast break the seal by producing gas that swells the lid.

Just because a jar is unopened, doesn't mean it is still safe. There are several ways to tell if an unopened jar of food has spoiled: If the jar looks swollen because the center of the lid is raised, it is probably bad. Lids should have a concave center. Food shouldn't still have rising air bubbles a couple days after canning either. This means it has not been properly sealed and air is somehow still getting in. The most obvious sign will be the discoloration of the product.

Mold is easy to spot and will look somewhat like cotton spores. When you open the jar make sure nothing is out of the ordinary. Don't just check the food either, something nasty could be hiding on the underside on the jar's lid. Mold can come in a variety of colors like green, white, blue, or black. Spurting liquid and foam can also be a sign of spoilage. Try not to inhale any of it before throwing it away. You can also smell if something's wrong. Even if everything looks fine, jars with unnatural odors should not be trusted.

Conclusion

You did it! You learned how to use a pressure canner safely. Congratulations, the horror stories stop with you. There aren't going to be any holes in your kitchen ceiling thanks to your smart choices. A pressure canner is no longer an object to fear, but instead an appliance for you to master. Now that you know how to properly prepare and can food products you no longer have to wait for your favorite veggies to go into season. Never again will your meat products spoil before you can consume it all. Throwing away leftovers will be a thing of the past.

Clearly, there is a lot to consider before you start your canning journey. Whatever size, brand, or model you choose, make sure you are comfortable with using it. The first step to safely using a pressure canner is to trust your appliance. If you have valid worries about the condition of your canner, don't use it. As cliche as it may be, always remember it is better to be safe than sorry. Modern pressure canners are built with your safety in mind, but that does not mean accidents can't happen. Know your model and its integral parts. That way, if something is wrong, you can easily identify and fix it before something bad happens.

Pressure canning isn't as difficult as it may seem. Once you get a hold of its process and precautions, it will be second nature. Always listen to the recipe, but first make sure it aligns with the USDA's food protocols. If it is telling you to pressure can strawberries, it is probably not a good recipe. In addition, being comfortable with the canning process does not mean being careless. Always be alert when the pressure canner is being used. Mistakes only happen when we let them, which means there's no reason to fear when we're being safe.

There are so many fun and interesting recipes you can use with a pressure canner. Once you've become comfortable with your model, feel free to be creative. While canning can be a job, it should also be enjoyable. Now that you know how to be safe when using your pressure canner there should be nothing stopping you from experimenting with different meals. There are so many avenues to explore whether it be with meat, broths, or vegetables. You can even learn how to use the water bath method with your pressure canner. Just make sure to thoroughly research the safety precautions and not just rely on what you know about the pressure canning method.

Lastly, thank you. Whether your pressure canning to make money or just for fun, you are helping to eliminate unwanted waste. Even if it's not on purpose, canning is still a sustainable lifestyle that helps the planet. The amount of produce that is thrown away everyday is almost sickening. Being mindful of what you use and what you need develops a healthy relationship with food and protects our environment. By making the decision to can, you are taking accountability for your waste and making a difference. Thanks to people like you, the world is becoming a better place. Good job!

Thank You

Dear reader, I would like to take this time to appreciate you.

Without your purchase and interest, I wouldn't be able to keep writing helpful books like this one.

Once again, THANK YOU for reading this book. I hope you enjoyed it as much as I enjoyed writing it.

Before you go, I have a small favor to ask of you. **Would you please consider posting a review of this book on the platform? Posting a review will help support the work of independent authors like me.**

Your feedback is very important and will help me continue to provide more informative literature in the future. I look forward to hearing from you.

>> Click here to leave a review on Amazon and see my other books on Food Preservation <<

References

Centers for Disease Control and Prevention. (2019). About botulism. CDC. https://www.cdc.gov/botulism/general.html

Chihak, S. (2020, April 6). Master pressure canning at home in 9 simple steps. Better Homes & Gardens. https://www.bhg.com/recipes/how-to/preserving-canning/pressure-canning-basics/#:~:text=A%20pressure%20canner%20is%20a

Chihak, S. (2020, April 27). Save your produce up to a year when you master water bath canning. Better Homes & Gardens. https://www.bhg.com/recipes/how-to/preserving-canning/canning-basics/

Cooks, C. (2020, July 22). All American vs Presto pressure canners. Corrie Cooks. https://www.corriecooks.com/all-american-vs-presto-pressure-canners/

Cash, J. (2015, December 22). Picking your pressure canner — All American or Presto? Backwoods Home Magazine. https://www.backwoodshome.com/picking-your-pressure-canner/

Fillmore Containers. (2015, August 7). Which jars are safe for pressure canning? (Updated). Fillmore Container. https://www.fillmorecontainer.com/blog/2015/08/07/which-jars-are-safe-for-pressure-canning/#:~:text=A%20Pressure%20Canner%20brings%20jar

Go Presto. (2019). Pressure canner care maintenance. Go Presto. https://www.gopresto.com/downloads/canning/PressureCannerCareandMaintenance.pdf

Healthy Canning. (n.d.). Pressure canner brands. Healthy Canning. https://www.healthycanning.com/pressure-canner-brands/#Typical_pressure_canner_brands

Meakin, C. (n.d.). Chicken vs. beef bone broth: Which is better for you. Bluebird Provisions. https://bluebirdprovisions.co/blogs/news/best-bone-broth

Meredith, L. (2020, September 17). Boiling water bath and pressure canning - When to use which. The Spruce Eats. https://www.thespruceeats.com/boiling-water-bath-versus-pressure-canning-1327438

National Center for Home Food Preservation. (2009). National Center for Home Food Preservation | How do I? Can meats. NCHFP. https://nchfp.uga.edu/how/can_05/strips_cubes_chunks.html

National Center for Home Food Preservation. (n.d.). National Center for Home Food Preservation | UGA Publications. NCHFP. https://nchfp.uga.edu/publications/uga/using_press_canners.html

Neal, J. (2015). Causes of pressure cooker explosions and how to avoid them. Watts Guerra LLP.

https://wattsguerra.com/product-liability-lawyers/causes-of-pressure-cooker-explosions-and-how-to-avoid-them/

Phelan, K. (2019, August 29). 4 canning dangers to be aware of. Homestead Survival Site. https://homesteadsurvivalsite.com/canning-dangers/

Philpotts, R. (2021, November 26). Top 7 health benefits of bone broth. BBC Good Food. https://www.bbcgoodfood.com/howto/guide/the-health-benefits-of-bone-broth

Preserve & Pickle. (2019, July 26). Buying a pressure canner - Guide to choosing & using a pressure canner. Preserve & Pickle. https://preserveandpickle.com/buying-a-pressure-canner-guide/#Considerations_When_Buying_A_Pressure_Canner

Rebekah. (2019, August 15). The ultimate list of what you can (and cannot!) can. J&R Pierce Family Farm. https://jrpiercefamilyfarm.com/2019/08/15/the-ultimate-list-of-what-you-can-and-cannot-can/

Sakawsky, A. (2021, August 9). How to use a pressure canner safely. The House & Homestead. https://thehouseandhomestead.com/how-to-use-a-pressure-canner-safely/

Schmutz, P., & Barefoot, S. (2011, August 20). Canning foods—The pH factor. Home & Garden Information Center | Clemson University, South Carolina. https://hgic.clemson.edu/factsheet/canning-foods-the-ph-factor/#:~:text=The%20acidity%2C%20or%20pH%2C%20of

Swanson, M. (2012). Using and caring for your pressure canner PNW 421. A Pacific Northwest Extension Publication. https://www.rollingprairie.k-state.edu/health-nutrition/food_preservation/Caring%20for%20your%20pressure%20canner.pdF

Thomas, C. (2021, February 10). Canning bone broth or stock (Chicken, beef, or vegetable). Homesteading Family. https://homesteadingfamily.com/how-to-can-broth/

Treadaway, A., & Crayton. (2019, May 21). Wise methods of canning vegetables. Alabama Cooperative Extension System. https://www.aces.edu/blog/topics/food-safety/wise-methods-of-canning-vegetables/

University of Illinois Extension. (n.d.). Storing vegetables - Taste of gardening - University of Illinois Extension. University of Illinois. https://web.extension.illinois.edu/tog/storing.cfm

Zepp, M. (2021, May 4). Canning jars and lids—An update. Penn State Extension. https://extension.psu.edu/canning-jars-and-lids-an-update

Made in United States
Orlando, FL
02 December 2023